# HOME REPAIR AND IMPROVEMENT

# ADVANCED WIRING

**TIME® LIFE BOOKS**

For information on and a full description
of any of the Time-Life Books series listed above,
please call 1-800-621-7026 or write:

Reader Information
Time-Life Customer Service
P.O. Box C-32068
Richmond Virginia 23261-2068

HOME REPAIR AND IMPROVEMENT

# ADVANCED WIRING

BY THE EDITORS OF TIME-LIFE BOOKS, ALEXANDRIA, VIRGINIA

*The Consultants*

Allen F. Andvik has been the technical
advisor at Skyvision, Inc. of Fergus Falls, MN,
since 1988. He is currently responsible for
customer product inserts and technical training
of all Skyvision employees on over 500 prod-
ucts. Mr. Andvik hosts *The Skyvision Show*
on C-Band satellite and has authored *The
Skyvision Do-It-Yourself Installation Manual.*

L.T. Bowden, Jr. has been a master electrician
and electrical contractor for 19 years, working in commercial, residential, and industrial
contracting, as well as specializing in residential electrical service work. He has been
an electrical-apprenticeship instructor for
the past nine years and is currently General
Manager of D & K Electric Inc., a contracting
firm in northern Virginia.

Joe Teets is a master electrician/contractor.
Currently in the Office of Adult and
Community Education for the Fairfax County
Public Schools, he has been involved in
apprenticeship training since 1985.

# CONTENTS

# 1

# Wiring for Modern Power and Control

New or old, your home's electrical system may not supply enough power to meet your needs. New appliances that cannot be installed without overloading a circuit, and breakers that trip or fuses that blow repeatedly are warning signs. You can solve these problems by expanding your service with more power, a new service panel or subpanel, or by running additional branch circuits from the panel.

Wiring a circuit breaker to a subpanel →

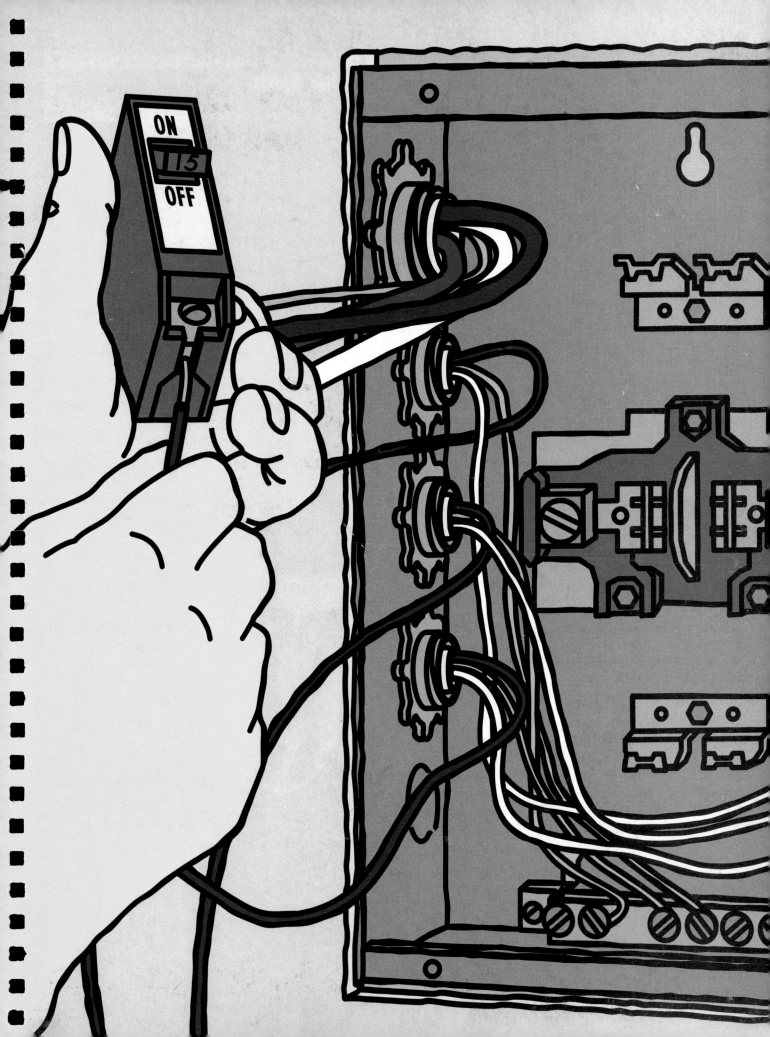

# Tools That Speed the Work

Although the wiring techniques described in this book go beyond the routine installation of an outlet or replacement of a light fixture, they do not necessarily require tools other than those in a basic kit. However, the more specialized tools pictured on these pages will speed and simplify advanced operations—particularly those involved in work on service panels and subpanels. These tools include cutters and rippers for large cables and conduit, special cable-pullers, and a number of testers that are more accurate and more versatile than the simple neon glow lamp.

## Precautions Before Starting to Work

The projects described in this book, such as connecting new circuits at the service panel and upgrading the service of an entire house, deal with potentially deadly current. But the work is no more dangerous than such basic wiring tasks as replacing a wall switch—if you take reasonable precautions. To protect yourself from injury, follow these rules:

✔ Always shut off power upstream before you begin a job. If you are working on a branch circuit, turn off the circuit breaker or pull the fuse—and label the service panel so no one will restore power. If you are working at the service panel, shut off power to it at the main disconnect (pages 62-64), have an electrician pull the meter (page 65), or have the utility company disconnect the power.

✔ Before you begin work, check the body of a fixture and every possible combination of wires with a voltage tester to make sure the power is off. If you find voltage or notice wires with damaged insulation, call in an electrician.

✔ Never work near live power. If you drill through a wall, fish wires between floors or along a wall, or work near a service drop, turn off electricity in the area.

✔ If your project is covered by an electrical permit, do not turn power on until an inspector approves your work.

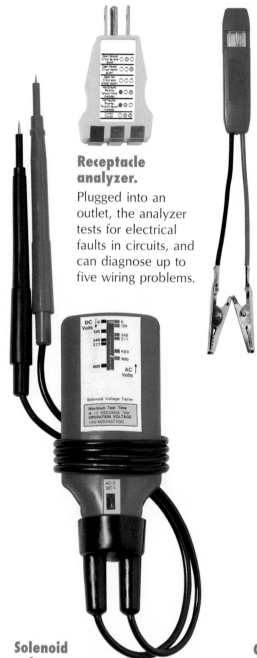

**Receptacle analyzer.**
Plugged into an outlet, the analyzer tests for electrical faults in circuits, and can diagnose up to five wiring problems.

**Low-voltage tester.**
Similar in appearance to its counterpart, the standard voltage tester, this tool is designed for checking stereo and other low-voltage circuits.

**Solenoid voltage tester.**
Used to ensure power has been shut off at a panel or a circuit and to check the wiring of 240-volt circuits, this tool measures voltages ranging from 120 to 600 volts. It has spring-loaded, retractable prongs that can be inserted into the slots of a receptacle or fixed in the open position for voltage tests in a panel or meter box. When extended from the tester body, the prongs can take a voltage reading on terminal lugs that are widely separated.

**Continuity tester.**
With a built-in battery that sends a small amount of current through a circuit, this device is used while power is turned off to detect problems within the circuit.

## Pipe cutters.

Though a hacksaw will cut heavy-wall conduit, a pipe cutter saves time and makes neater cuts. A carbide wheel in the head of the metal-cutting tool *(top)* cuts a groove as the tool is rotated around the conduit; it is tightened with each revolution until it cuts clear through. The plastic-pipe cutter *(bottom)* has handles that are squeezed, activating a blade that severs the pipe.

## Wire basket.

The most convenient way to secure wire and cable to the end of a fish tape is with a wire basket. A cylinder woven of thin steel strands, it squeezes tight around a wire in its mouth when the tape is pulled.

## Electrician's knife.

This folding knife has a safety lock to keep it from closing in use. The hooked portion of the blade is particularly useful for stripping insulation in the tight confines of a panel or meter box; the straight part of the blade is used to strip insulation from heavy cable before it is connected.

## Coax-cable crimper.

With this tool, you can cut coax cable and attach F-connectors to it. When squeezed, the crimper crushes the end of the connector, securing it to the cable.

## Cable ripper.

A metal clip 4 to 5 inches long with a sharp tooth inside its body, the ripper fits over flexible cable up to $\frac{5}{8}$ inch in diameter to slice through the sheathing neatly and quickly. The handle sometimes contains a wire gauge.

## Fish tape.

A fish tape with a grip built into the body is superior to conventional tapes for pulling service cable or thick bunches of wire around corners and through sharp conduit bends. The body of the spool turns independently of the handle for extra pulling power, and the handle can be used to rewind the tape.

The kind of cable you need for power supplies—120 and 240 volts—and for lights and appliances depends on three factors: the purpose of the circuit; the number of amperes of current to be carried; and the location of the cable.

**Service Entrance Concentric (SEC):** Used between overhead power company lines and a house's electric meter, SEC cable also connects the meter to a service panel's fuses or circuit breakers, or to a main disconnect *(pages 62-64)*. The cable is called concentric because the bare strands of wire that serve as its neutral conductor are wrapped completely around an inner core consisting of two black insulated hot wires, or one black and one red.

**Service Entrance Round (SER):** SER cable runs from a main disconnect to a service panel and is also used for range and clothes-dryer circuits. SER cable is as large as SEC cable and contains two hot wires, but has bare ground wires twisted together into a single thick bundle and one white or gray neutral wire.

**Nonmetallic (NM):** In relatively small 12- and 14-gauge sizes, this cable serves the 15- and 20-ampere interior branch circuits that supply light fixtures and receptacles for small appliances. In sizes 10-gauge and larger, NM cable serves large appliances and subpanels. These large cables contain either two or three conductors. Three-conductor cable, with one white conductor and the others either black or black and red, is most often used as feeder cable for subpanels and for 120/240 volt range circuits. Large two-conductor cable is used for appliances such as heaters that require only 240-volt current.

**Underground Feeder (UF):** Sheathed in tough, moisture-proof plastic, UF cable can be buried underground. Like NM cable, it can contain either two or three conductors. It comes in an especially wide range of sizes. The smallest is used for individual branch circuits, while larger sizes run between a main service panel and subpanel in a garage or outbuilding. The largest of all, called underground service entrance (USE) cable, can connect a meter to underground power lines.

**Armored:** Containing the same sizes of conductors as UF and NM cable, armored cable is sheathed with a spiral steel jacket. It is not as flexible as plastic-sheathed cable, but must be used when wiring is buried in mortar or secured to a surface that is especially vulnerable to damage.

**Choosing Cable:** Once you have chosen the kind of cable you need for a wiring job, you can determine the exact size to buy. The maximum current for every size is strictly limited by the electrical code, which prescribes formulas for calculating wire sizes depending on the type of circuit and the load on it *(pages 123-125)*.

## AN ARRAY OF CABLES

Each of these cables has special properties that suit it for its function in a home electrical system. Service entrance cables, both SEC and SER, have thick, tough outer sheathings to resist moisture and fire. The sheathing of UF cable is also fungus- and corrosion-resistant, and fills the space inside the cable so the individual wires run in separate channels. NM cable combines lightweight plastic sheathing and thin wires to make an inexpensive product that can easily be snaked inside walls. Armored cable is wrapped with a steel jacket for protection.

While the colors and characteristics of the outer sheathing vary widely from cable to cable, the insulation covering the conductors inside the sheathing follows a single code: Hot wires are red or black, neutral wires are white or gray, and ground wires are green or bare. The only exceptions to the rule occur in SEC cable, which uses a bare wire for neutral rather than for ground. In some switch circuits, the white wire may be hot—but any white wire used in this way can be recoded as black with paint or tape where it enters a box.

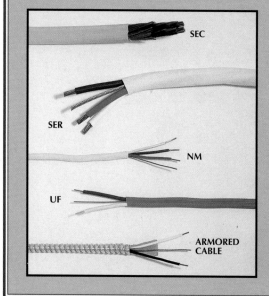

When the price of copper soared in the early 1960s, manufacturers began making residential wires from aluminum or copper-clad aluminum. Though the copper-coated type proved safe, pure aluminum wiring may be dangerous. The hazard of aluminum wiring arises from two types of corrosion. One occurs when aluminum is connected to a dissimilar metal such as the copper-alloy terminals of a fixture. The other is oxidization of aluminum when it is exposed to air after its insulation is stripped.

Both reactions increase the resistance in the wiring, making it hotter when in use and a greater fire hazard.

Corrosion can be prevented if the wiring is installed in exact accordance with the National Electrical Code. If your house's wiring is pure aluminum—the wires are dull gray and the sheathing is marked AL—all receptacles, switches, and other electrical devices must be marked CO/ALR. Avoid using high-wattage appliances in rarely occupied rooms and look for warning signs such as warm cover plates, devices that fail for no apparent reason, and strange odors or smoke.

**⚠ CAUTION** *Never attempt to repair or improve an aluminum-wired system yourself, except for replacing switches or receptacles with ones marked CO/ALR. Such a project should be done only by a licensed electrician. Never try to install a ground-fault circuit interrupter (pages 56-57) in a system with aluminum wires; consult an electrican.*

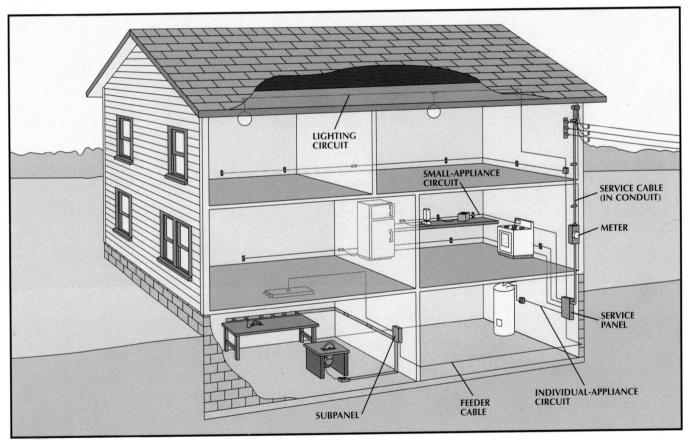

LIGHTING CIRCUIT

SMALL-APPLIANCE CIRCUIT

SERVICE CABLE (IN CONDUIT)

METER

SERVICE PANEL

INDIVIDUAL-APPLIANCE CIRCUIT

FEEDER CABLE

SUBPANEL

### The right cable for every job.

The drawing above shows every type of cable likely to be found in a home; the wiring of the circuits has been simplified for clarity. The largest line is the service cable that carries power from the overhead power lines, through the meter, to the service panel in the basement. All the other cables in the house branch out from there. The feeder cable running to the subpanel in the basement workshop is large enough to handle all the loads wired to the subpanel. Two individual-appliance circuits serve high-amperage equipment: heavy two-conductor cable supplies 240 volts to the water heater; a four-wire SER cable supplies a 120/240-volt circuit to the electric range, which needs 240 volts for its heating elements and 120 volts for its light and clock. Two small-appliance circuits, wired with 12-gauge cable to carry 20 amps, power groups of receptacles. One circuit serves the refrigerator and extends to the dining room, where table-top appliances might be used; the other provides the kitchen work space with receptacles. A general lighting circuit, the most common type of all, is wired with 14-gauge cable to provide 15 amperes for the upstairs light fixtures and several receptacles.

Whether a project involves a simple circuit extension or the addition of a completely new circuit, you likely will need to route wiring through one or more walls. Passing cable through an interior wall, which is hollow, is relatively simple. But running wire through an exterior wall, which is probably packed with insulation, sealed by vapor barriers, and blocked by bracing and fire stops—short pieces of wood set horizontally between studs to retard the spread of flame—can be more complicated. Solid masonry walls can be problematic as well.

**Dodging Obstacles:** The easiest way to get past the obstacles of an exterior wall is to avoid them, taking wires up through an unused chimney or alongside the plumbing vent stack *(pages 86-87)*, which rises from floor to floor through holes that are generally larger than the stack piping. In a wall of concrete blocks, wire can be fished through the hollow cores of the blocks *(opposite)*. In addition to these tricks, a direct attack works on a frame exterior wall. The clogged spaces between its studs are not always completely impassable—wire can be run between the vapor barrier and the back of the wallboard. When you hit a firestop or brace, you can cut a hole through the wallboard and chisel a notch in the obstruction, then cover the wire with a metal plate and patch the hole *(pages 15-16)*. And if long runs or the vapor barrier make it difficult to tell when two fish tapes meet, you can wire them to an electric bell that will ring when the tapes touch *(opposite)*.

**Pulling Wire:** Once a fish tape extends along to the full length of a cable run, hook cables to it in the conventional way or use a basket *(page 17)* to pull many wires at once. While you pull the tape back, have a helper push the cables or wires at the far end—the extra force will help move them past obstructions. Always pull enough cable to provide at least 6 inches of slack in every junction box, plus plenty of extra for trimming and stripping.

**TOOLS**

| | |
|---|---|
| Fish tape | Wire basket |
| Hammer | Cable strippers |
| Ball-peen hammer | Pliers |
| Wood chisel | Electrician's knife |
| Cold chisel | Diagonal cutting pliers |
| Keyhole saw | Long-nose pliers |
| Electric drill and bits | Multipurpose tool |
| Wire cutters | Utility knife |
| | Tin snips |
| | Pry bar |

**MATERIALS**

| | |
|---|---|
| Electrical cable | Insulated wire (18-gauge) |
| Dry-cell battery (6-volt) | Metal plate ($\frac{1}{16}$") |
| Doorbell | Roofing nails (1") |
| Alligator clips | Patching mortar |
| | Electrical tape |

**SAFETY TIPS**

*Protect your eyes with goggles when using power tools, hammering, or cutting through wallboard.*

# FISHING WIRE THROUGH WALLS

### Belling a fish tape.
◆ Cut access holes at the top and bottom of the wall with a keyhole saw.
◆ With a helper, feed a fish tape into the wall at each opening.
◆ Hook a terminal of a 6-volt dry-cell battery to one terminal of an inexpensive doorbell.
◆ Run an 18-gauge insulated wire from the other battery terminal to one of the fish tapes and fasten it with an alligator clip.
◆ Run a wire from the other bell terminal to the second fish tape.
◆ Feed the ends of the tapes together *(right)*— when they touch, the bells will sound.

DRY-CELL BATTERY · DOORBELL

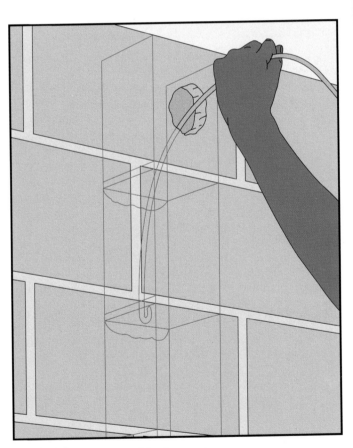

### Fishing in concrete block.
◆ With a ball-peen hammer and cold chisel, punch a hole into a concrete block at the top of the wall in line with the hollow cores of all the blocks to the bottom of the wall.
◆ Punch a similar hole at the bottom of the wall.
◆ Into the upper hole, push a fish tape down through the hollow cores of the blocks below *(above)*.
◆ Have a helper feed another fish tape upward from the lower hole. If either tape meets an obstruction such as mortar, flip the tape in a half circle, using its natural curl to turn the head toward the opposite side of the block. Keep twisting the tapes until you can hook them together.

If one or two courses at the top of a wall are made of solid block, you must use armored cable:
◆ Fish the cables through a hole punched into the hollow cores at the bottom of the wall and another below the solid blocks.
◆ Chisel a notch in the solid blocks, run armored cable through the wall and in the notch, and cover both the cable and the notch with patching mortar *(page 21)*.

⚠ **CAUTION** *If you find any signs of moisture on the surface of the wall or inside the blocks, use NMC or UF nonmetallic sheathed cable—both approved for damp locations.*

**Using an I-beam.**
To make a long cable run between opposite masonry walls, you can often take advantage of a boxed I-beam.
◆ Remove a section of wallboard and push a fish tape through *(above)*.
◆ Use the curl of the fish tape to keep the hook against the I-beam and away from the strips that support the wallboard.

# RUNNING CABLE AROUND A DOOR

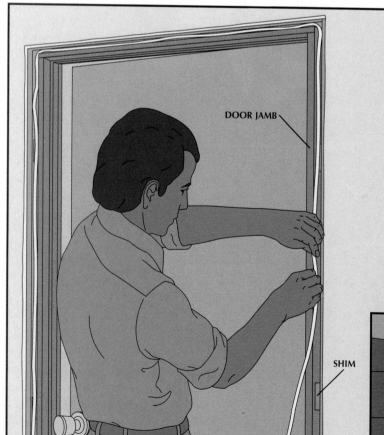

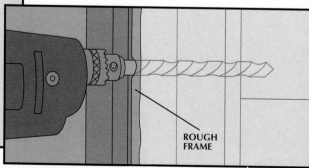

**Routing the wiring.**
◆ Remove the door casing.
◆ With a sharp chisel, split away part of the shims that hold the jambs in place, being careful not to change the relative positions of the paired shims and thus twist the door frame.
◆ Lay in the cable *(left)* so it will sit at least $1\frac{1}{4}$ inches from the outer edge of the jamb. If the wiring will be less than $1\frac{1}{4}$ inches from the edge, cover it with metal kickplates *(page 16, Step 3)* along its length.
◆ Replace the trim, angling the nails to avoid hitting the cable.

To run cable through an exterior door frame, use a long bit to drill a hole through the rough frame, between shims, at a 45-degree angle away from the door *(inset)*.

# NOTCHING A WOODEN OBSTRUCTION

## 1. Exposing the obstruction.

When a firestop or brace prevents you from running cable vertically behind wallboard, you can notch the obstruction and pass the cable around it.

◆ With a drill and a spade bit slightly larger than the tip of a keyhole saw, bore four holes through the wall around the obstruction midway between the adjacent studs, forming a rectangle.

◆ Starting at one of the upper holes, saw away the wallboard within the rectangle *(right)*. Avoid cutting the firestop or brace.

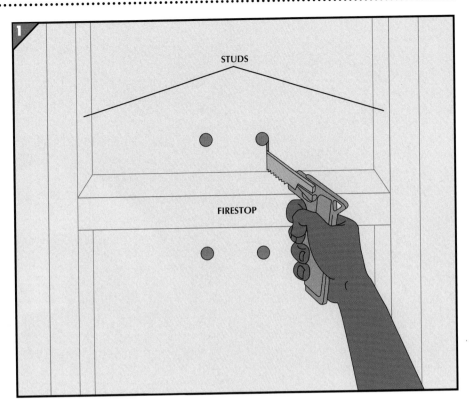

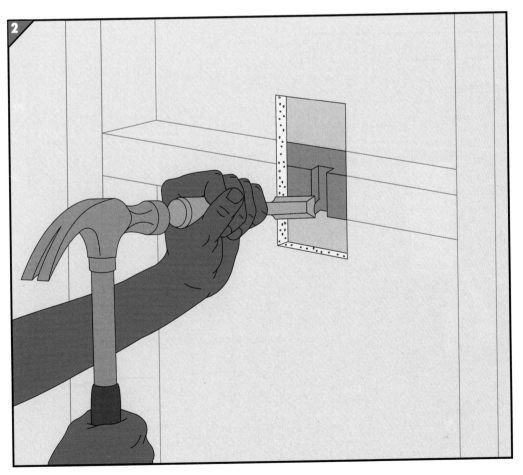

## 2. Cutting the notch.

◆ Hold a wood chisel against the firestop or brace, centered between the edges of the access hole, and tap the handle with a hammer to cut a notch large enough to hold the cable without pinching it *(left)*.

◆ Run the cable through the notch.

## 3. Protecting the cable.

The electrical code requires that cable run less than $1\frac{1}{4}$ inches from the back of wallboard be protected with a metal plate $\frac{1}{16}$ inch thick.

◆ Hold a metal kickplate—available at electrical-supply stores—on the firestop or brace across the cable and hammer it in place *(right)*. The teeth on the plate's back face *(photograph)* will anchor it to the wood. If the plate has holes near the ends, drive a 1-inch roofing nail through each one.

◆ Patch the wall.

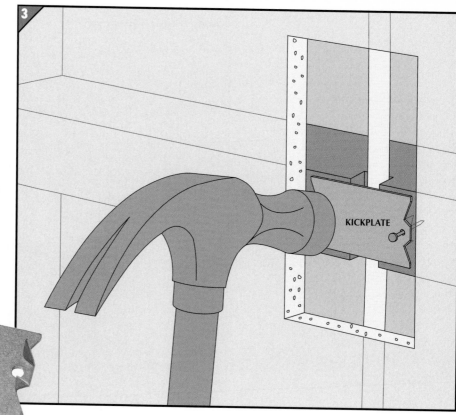

KICKPLATE

TEETH

# CUTTING INTO PLASTER AND LATH WALLS

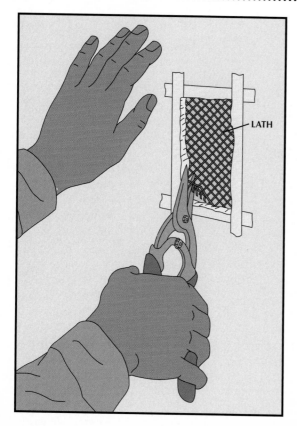

LATH

**Making an opening.**

◆ Outline the opening on the wall and apply masking tape around it to keep the plaster from chipping badly.

◆ Score the outline several times with a utility knife.

◆ With a cold chisel and a ball-peen hammer, gently remove all of the plaster within the outline until the metal lath beneath is completely exposed.

◆ With tin snips, cut away the metal lath from the hole in the plaster *(left)*. Work carefully; flexing the lath may crumble the plaster around the edges of the hole.

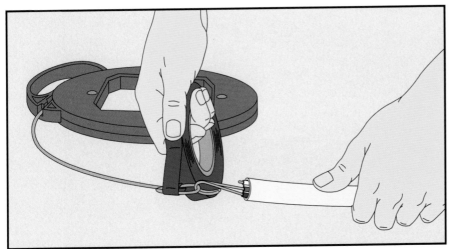

### Fishing a large NM cable.
◆ To avoid a bulky fish-tape connection that snags at obstructions, first strip 2 inches of the sheathing from a cable *(page 18)* and cut off the end of one of the wires—in this example, the white neutral wire.
◆ Strip the insulation from the ends of the two remaining wires *(page 19)* and loop the bare conductors over the fish tape.
◆ Wind electrical tape over the entire connection, beginning at the fish tape and tapering the turns of the tape over the sheathing of the cable *(left)*.

### Using a wire basket.
Although some fish tapes are de-signed to pull more than one cable, you can also pull several small ca-bles at one time with a wire basket on the end of a standard fish tape.
◆ Hook the basket to the end of the tape.
◆ Compress the basket by pushing the mouth toward its eye hook and insert the cables *(right)*. The basket will tighten around the cables as it is pulled.

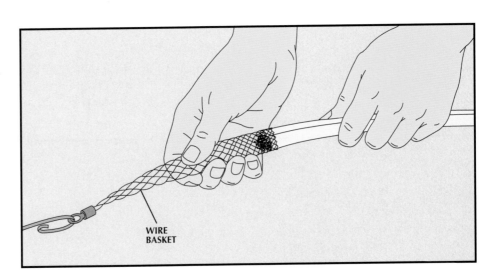

WIRE BASKET

**TRICKS OF THE TRADE**

## Pulling Cable Through Corners and Tight Spots

To pull cable around a corner, drill two holes at the same height through the outside faces of the two adjoining studs. Locate the holes at least $1\frac{1}{4}$ inches from either edge of the studs. Bend the cable at 90 de-grees a few inches from the end and push it into one of the holes. You can then use long-nose pliers to reach into the other hole and pull out the cable *(right)*.

To fish cable through a narrow spot, wrap electrical tape around the fish-tape connection as described above, and spread cable-pulling lubricant over the tape. The lubricant will help ease the cable through the tight space.

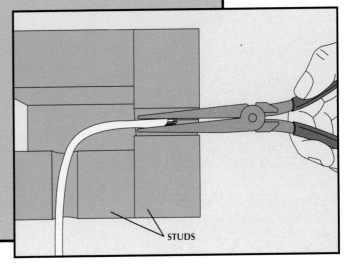

STUDS

# THE RIGHT WAY TO STRIP CABLE

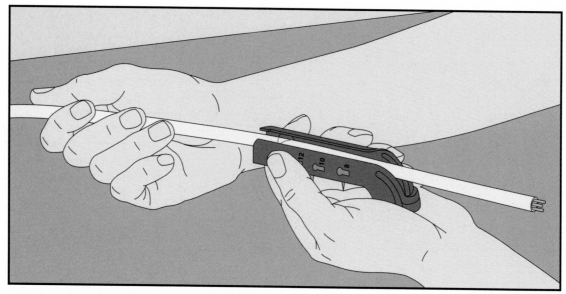

### NM cable.
You can use a knife or pliers to strip NM cable, but a cable ripper makes the job easy.
◆ Close the cable ripper around the cable so the tooth pierces the sheathing *(above)*, then pull hard to slide the ripper to the end of the cable.
◆ Peel the sheathing back and cut it off with pliers.

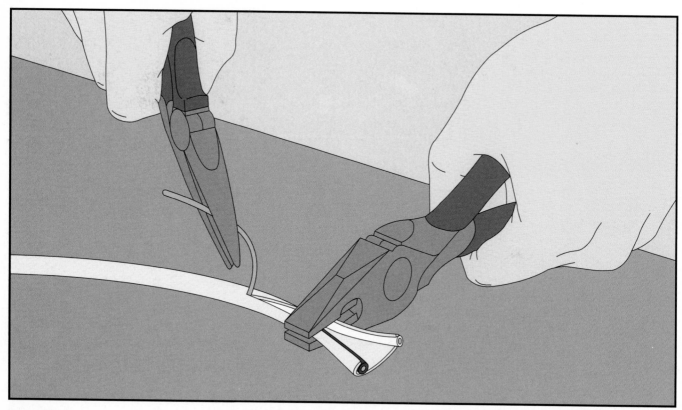

### UF cable.
◆ Cut 1 inch of cable sheathing open with a cable stripper or diagonal cutters.
◆ Bend the end of the bare ground wire out of the sheathing, then grasp the sheathing with one pair of pliers and the ground wire with another and pull the ground wire upward to rip the sheathing *(above)*.

To strip the insulation from the individual wires, you can pull the sheathing from each one in the same way and cut off the sheathing, or use a multipurpose tool *(opposite)*.

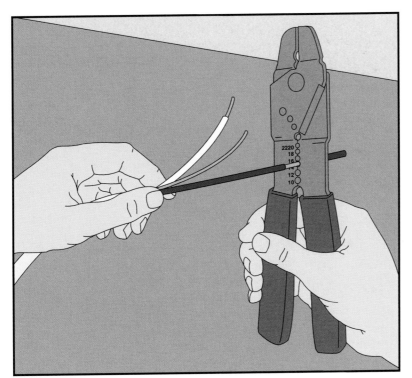

## Stripping insulation from wires.

◆ Match the gauge of the wire you are working with—it is printed on the plastic sheathing of the cable—to the corresponding wire-stripping hole in a multipurpose tool.

◆ Close the tool over the wire $\frac{1}{2}$ inch to $\frac{3}{4}$ inch from the end and rotate the tool a quarter-turn in each direction.

◆ Without opening the tool, pull the severed insulation off the wire to expose the bare metal *(left)*.

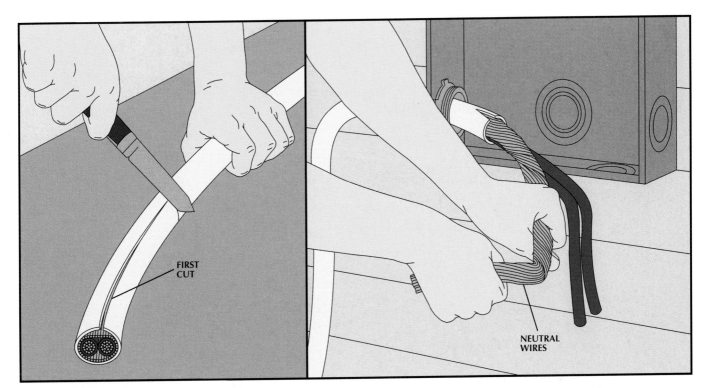

FIRST CUT

NEUTRAL WIRES

## SEC and SER cable.

◆ Set the cable (SEC cable is pictured above) on a flat surface and, with an electrician's knife, make one cut along the sheathing and another around the cable at the base of the first *(above, left)*.

◆ Pull the sheathing back and cut it off.

◆ To prepare the cable for connection after feeding it into a service-panel box, bunch the neutral wires to one side of the cable, bend 6 inches of those wires at a right angle, and use the bent portion as a handle to twist the strands together *(above, right)*.

◆ Cut off the bend with diagonal cutting pliers, and trim the twisted portion as needed.

# Putting Outlets in Tight Places

The basic components of a branch circuit—outlet boxes in which electrical connections are made, and devices such as switches and receptacles that are mounted in them—have been standardized for decades. Specially sized or shaped boxes and devices, and uncommon mounting techniques, are available to meet various installation problems.

**Special Boxes and Devices:** The standard outlet box, ranging from $2\frac{1}{2}$ to $3\frac{1}{2}$ inches deep, serves well for most construction and remodeling. To locate switches or receptacles in unlikely spots, you can turn to special shallow or deep boxes. A shallow box, for example, may fit into a notch cut

in a stud or a hollow chiseled in masonry *(page 21)*.

Uncommon switches and receptacles are also available. Called interchangeables *(box, below)*, they are so small that three can be mounted where only one or two normal devices would fit *(pages 22-23)*.

**Plastic Boxes:** Before 1970, nearly all outlet boxes were made of metal; today, less expensive plastic boxes are increasingly common. The two materials are interchangeable, but because plastic will not conduct electricity, the boxes cannot be grounded. Instead, the devices in them are grounded with wire-cap connections and jumper wires *(page 24)*. In every

other respect, follow the standard procedures for installing a new circuit. Run the cable for the circuit before mounting the boxes, then connect and ground the devices, check the circuit *(pages 45-47)* and wire it to the service panel or subpanel *(pages 32-41)*.

⚠ **CAUTION** *Never work on a live circuit: Switch off power to it at the service panel, then check all wires with a voltage tester (page 36).*

⚠ **CAUTION** *If your house has aluminum wiring (page 11), use receptacles and switches marked CO/ALR.*

---

 **TOOLS**

Electric drill
Wood chisel
Keyhole saw
Screwdriver
Cold chisel
Ball-peen hammer
Mason's trowel
Drive pin set

 **MATERIALS**

Outlet boxes
NM cable
Plaster ring
Premixed mortar
Metal clamp and drive pin
Steel wool
Wood shims
Armored cable
Wire caps
Interchangeable devices
Jumper wire

 **SAFETY TIPS**

*Protect your eyes with goggles when using power tools or hammering. Wear gloves and goggles when working with mortar.*

---

## INTERCHANGEABLE DEVICES

These switches and receptacles have the same depth as their standard counterparts and are wired the same way *(pages 22-23)*, but are so small that three can be mounted where only one or two normal devices would fit. The box they are installed in is larger to accommodate the extra cables, and is fitted with a special windowed plate called a plaster ring *(page 22)* to adapt it for the interchangeables.

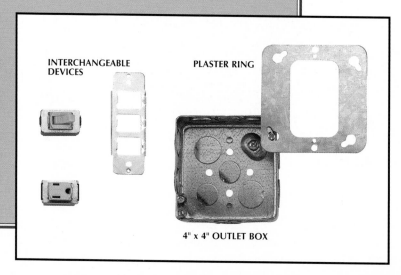

INTERCHANGEABLE DEVICES

PLASTER RING

4" x 4" OUTLET BOX

## Notching a stud.

◆ Expose the stud *(page 15, Step 1)*, cutting a hole in the wallboard the same size as a shallow box.

◆ Drill two rows of small holes $\frac{3}{4}$ inch deep into the top and bottom of the exposed wood *(right)*. Angle the top holes slightly upward and the bottom holes slightly downward.

◆ Chisel away the wood between the holes.

◆ Draw the cables into the box and screw the box to the stud, mounting it horizontally so the cables can clear the stud.

⚠ **CAUTION** *When cutting into walls or ceilings, take precautions against releasing lead and asbestos particles into the air (page 12).*

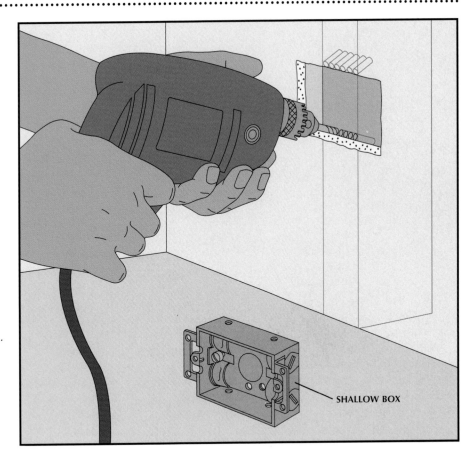

SHALLOW BOX

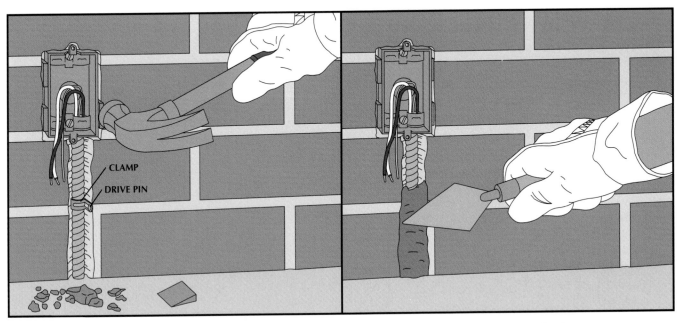

CLAMP

DRIVE PIN

## Mounting a box in masonry.

◆ Trace a shallow box on the wall and chip away the brick within the outline with a cold chisel and a ball-peen hammer, cutting an opening as deep as the box.

◆ Chisel a V-shaped groove along the wall to the box to accommodate a run of armored cable, then run the armored cable into the box.

◆ Place the box in the opening so the front is flush with the wall.

◆ Secure the cable to the wall with a drive pin and a clamp *(page 67, Step 4)*.

◆ Tap tapered wood shims in around the box to wedge it in place *(above, left)*

◆ With a mason's trowel, cover the cable with mortar tinted to match the wall *(above, right)*.

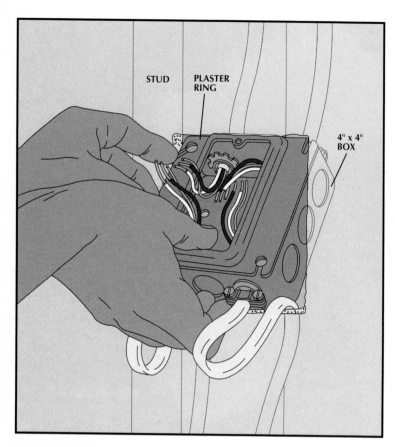

STUD    PLASTER RING

4" x 4" BOX

### Flush-mounting with a plaster ring.
◆ For a box that will contain interchangeable devices *(page 20)*, buy a model that is large enough to accommodate the number of cables it will serve. Cut a hole *(page 15, Step 1)* as wide as the box and 1 inch taller through the wallboard next to a stud.
◆ Clamp the cables in the box, fit it with a plaster ring, and angle the box into the hole so the ring is flush with the wall surface *(left)*.
◆ Screw the box to the stud.
◆ After installing the devices *(below and opposite)*, fill the gap between the plaster ring and the wall with steel wool and patching plaster.

⚠ **CAUTION**    *When cutting into walls or ceilings, take precautions against releasing lead and asbestos particles into the air* (page 12).

# SPACESAVING SWITCHES AND RECEPTACLES

### Fastening components to a strap.
◆ To assemble an interchangeable device, fit a tongue of the strap into the matching slot in a device such as switch or receptacle.
◆ Bend the T-slot opposite the tongue with a screwdriver to grip the device *(right)*.

If you want to remove an interchangeable device, twist the T-slot in the opposite direction to loosen its grip.

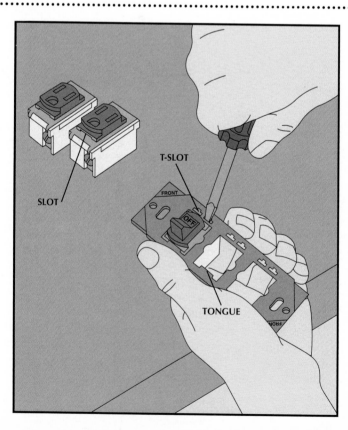

SLOT

T-SLOT

FRONT

TONGUE

## Two receptacles and a switch.

◆ To control one receptacle with a switch while the other remains supplied with power from a second circuit, first join the incoming and outgoing black leads of the first circuit with a wire cap, then run a black jumper from the cap to one terminal of the switch.

◆ Connect the other terminal of the switch to the brass terminal of a receptacle with a jumper.

◆ Join the incoming and outgoing neutral leads with a wire cap and connect them to the silver terminal of the receptacle with a white jumper.

◆ Wire the other receptacle into the second circuit as you would a standard receptacle.

◆ With a large wire cap, join the ground wires of both circuits, and run green insulated or bare copper jumpers from the cap to the green grounding terminals of the receptacles and to a grounding screw in the box.

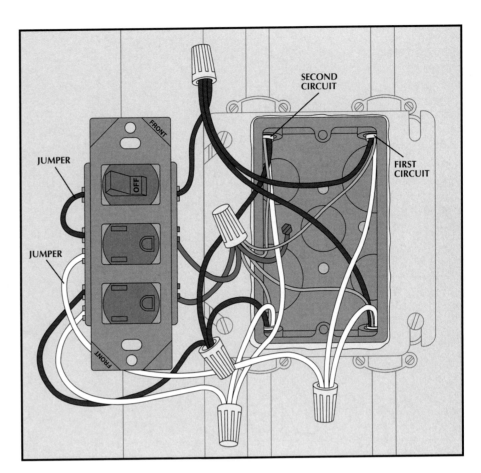

## Two switches and a receptacle.

◆ To control a fixture in one circuit with the top switch, while the bottom switch controls a receptacle in a second circuit, first wire the top switch into the fixture circuit.

◆ With a wire cap, join the incoming and outgoing black leads of the second circuit, and run a black jumper from the cap to a terminal on the bottom switch.

◆ Run a second black jumper from the bottom switch terminal to the brass terminal of the receptacle.

◆ With a wire cap, join the incoming and outgoing neutral leads of the circuit with a jumper wire that connects to the silver terminal of the receptacle.

◆ Join all the bare copper wires and link them with a jumper to a grounding screw on the box and the grounding terminal on the receptacle.

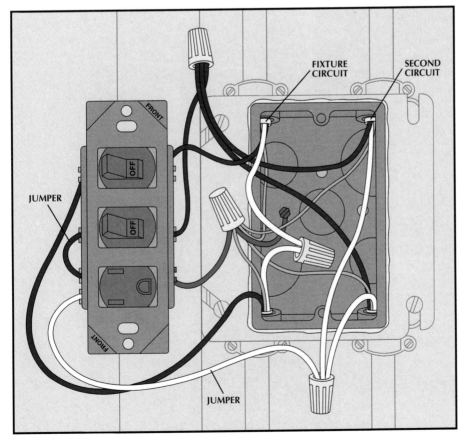

# GROUNDING PLASTIC BOXES

### In a wall box.

◆ Join the incoming and outgoing ground wire leads with a jumper, and secure them with a wire cap. Run the jumper to the green grounding terminal on the device—in this example, a switch.

◆ Make the other connections the standard way: Attach the incoming and outgoing black leads to the brass terminals of the switch and join the incoming and outgoing white leads.

> ⚠ **CAUTION** *To ground a switch correctly in a plastic box, buy a switch that comes with a separate grounding connection, identifiable by a green screw terminal. Do not ground a switch with a connection to its strap or mounting screws.*

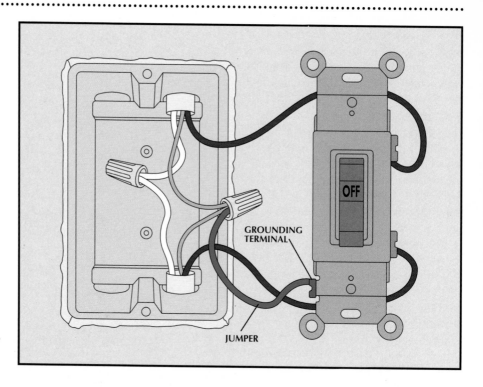

GROUNDING TERMINAL

JUMPER

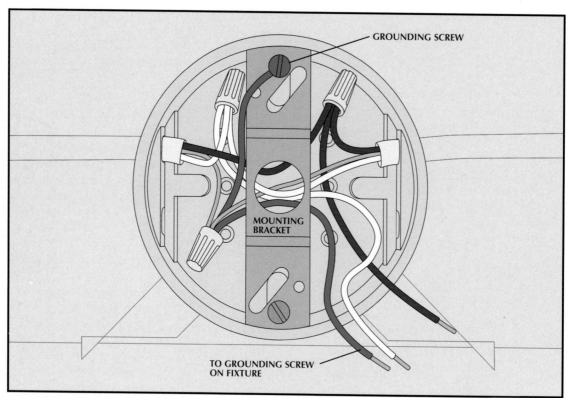

GROUNDING SCREW

MOUNTING BRACKET

TO GROUNDING SCREW ON FIXTURE

### In a ceiling box.

◆ Join the incoming and outgoing ground leads and connect two jumpers to them with a wire cap.

◆ Run one of the jumpers to the grounding screw on the light fixture, the other to a grounding screw on the mounting bracket

of the box. If the box has a grounding strap, connect the second jumper to it instead of to the mounting bracket.

◆ Join the incoming and outgoing black leads with one cap and the white neutral leads with another, and run jumpers from the caps to the fixture.

## The controversy over grounding.

It was not until the early 1950s that electricians began adding grounds to electrical circuits in any systematic way. Occasionally, conscientious wiremen would wrap a scrap of wire between an outlet box and a water pipe, and in 1955 this practice was made mandatory by the National Electrical Code. Later, the code decreed that any outlet within 8 feet of a cold-water pipe had to be connected to the pipe with a ground wire—but the rule did not specify how to make the connection. Many electricians tucked the wire under a cable clamp or any other handy protrusion in the box, and taped or twisted it around the pipe.

In the early 1960s both the U.S. and Canadian codes tightened their grounding requirements. Three-hole receptacles with separate grounding terminals were mandated for kitchens, bathrooms, and laundries—they are now required in all rooms —and the correct grounding connections were spelled out for the first time. No longer could any nearby pipe be used; the grounds had to terminate in the service panel. And no longer could ground wires merely be twisted together and pushed into a box—they had to be pressure-connected with either a wire cap or a bonding screw.

The choice between a cap and a screw is not as simple as it may seem, for while the U.S. and Canada have standardized their connection methods, the two countries are in disagreement on this question.

Canada frowns upon the use of wire caps and jumpers; its code suggests that the ground wire be looped around a bonding screw, then connected to the grounding terminal on the device *(right, top)*. The U.S. code requires caps and jumpers *(right, bottom)*. Most electricians believe that both methods work but doubt that the conflict will ever be resolved. The Canadian code writers contend that wire caps can come loose and the pigtailed wires inside them can come apart; their U.S. counterparts argue that a wire grounded to a screw can break.

Whatever the connection method, experts in both countries predict that grounding requirements will continue to grow more stringent. Grounded switches, now used mainly in plastic boxes, will probably be required universally, and the use of ground-fault circuit interrupters (GFCIs) *(page 56)* will almost certainly be expanded.

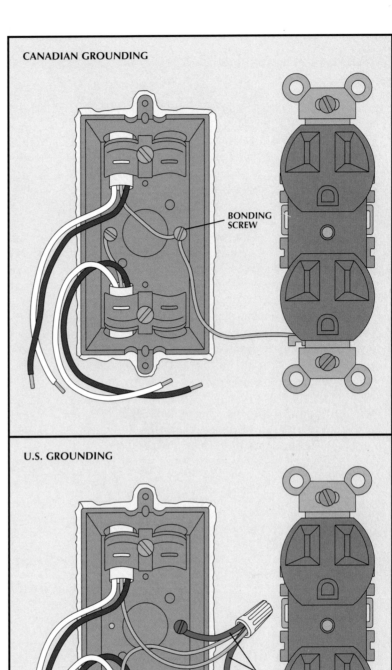

CANADIAN GROUNDING

BONDING SCREW

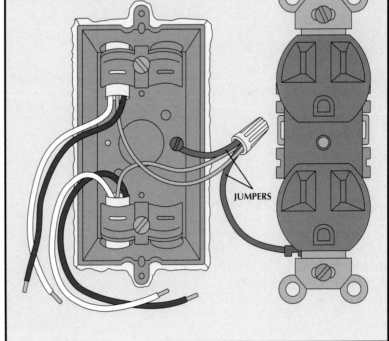

U.S. GROUNDING

JUMPERS

# Surface Wiring: The Easiest Way to Add a Circuit

There is no simpler way to run a new circuit in your home than by using raceway—interlocking channels that run along the outsides of walls and floors, housing receptacles and switches. Raceway is best suited for garages, workshops, or other dry locations where concealing wires is impractical or where you may want to change or add to a circuit later.

Compact Raceway: The metal raceway shown on these pages, available in kits, combines high wire-carrying capacity with compactness—the receptacles and switches are located inside the raceway channel, not in full-sized, obtrusive boxes. Installation begins with attaching base pieces to the floor or wall. The pieces can be cut with a fine-tooth hacksaw and come with regularly spaced knockouts for flat-head screws. Wires are laid in the base and protective U-shaped wire clips are set over them at 1-foot intervals. In one type of raceway, the switches and receptacles are wired and set in position at any location you please *(page 28)*, and the covers are snapped into place over the base. Another type, which comes with receptacles prewired at regular intervals, can be partially disguised by recessing it in

the wallboard along the floor in place of a baseboard *(page 30)*. For both types, special base and cover pieces route raceway around corners and connect it to the electrical system. You may be able to add wires to an existing raceway *(page 31)*, but check the manufacturer's specifications and the electrical code first.

Energizing the Circuit: You can attach a new raceway circuit to a service panel with a fitting called an offset connector *(below)* or to an outlet box with a fitting called an adapter plate *(opposite, top)*. Be sure that the base pieces in the system are securely fastened to one another. The base pieces are designed to form a continuous ground from every part of the raceway system back to the service panel or outlet box.

> ⚠ **CAUTION** *Never work on a live circuit: Switch off power to it at the service panel, then check all wires with a voltage tester (page 36).*

> ⚠ **CAUTION** *If your house has aluminum wiring (page 11), have a specially trained, licensed electrician install the new circuit.*

---

 **TOOLS**

Screwdriver
Hacksaw
Wire strippers
Voltage tester

Diagonal
  cutting pliers
Hammer
Drywall saw
Pry Bar

 **MATERIALS**

Chase nipple and
  lock nut
Wire caps

Raceway kit
Jumper wires
  (black, white,
  and green)
Electrician's tape

Wood block
Quarter-round
  molding
Wood glue
Finishing nails (1½")

 **SAFETY TIPS**

*Wear goggles
when hammering.*

---

# CONNECTING TO THE POWER SOURCE

**Tapping into a service panel.**
◆ Turn off the power to the panel *(pages 62-65)*, then remove matching knockouts from the panel box *(pages 37-38, Steps 1-3)* and an offset connector base.
◆ Screw the connector base to the wall so the knockout holes in the panel and base align *(right)*.
◆ Fasten the connector base to the panel box with a lock nut and a terminal adapter called a chase nipple. The circuit wires will run through this nipple, but do not wire the circuit to the panel until all other connections have been made and you have covered the base with the offset connector cover *(page 28, Step 4)*.

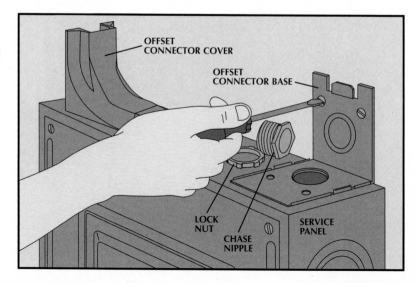

OFFSET CONNECTOR COVER
OFFSET CONNECTOR BASE
LOCK NUT
CHASE NIPPLE
SERVICE PANEL

## Tapping into an outlet.

◆ Turn off the power to the circuit, then disconnect the receptacle from the box.

◆ Join the wires in the box: white to white, black to black, and ground to ground and, with wire caps, add new lengths of matching wire, each 8 to 10 inches long.

◆ Thread the three new wires through the raceway adapter plate (right), push the other connections into the box, and screw on the plate.

◆ Thread the wires through the knock-out holes of a raceway base, fit the knockout over the nipple, and fasten the nipple lock washer and bushing.

To restore power to the tapped circuit before completing the raceway system, cap the bare ends of the raceway wires with wire caps and electrician's tape.

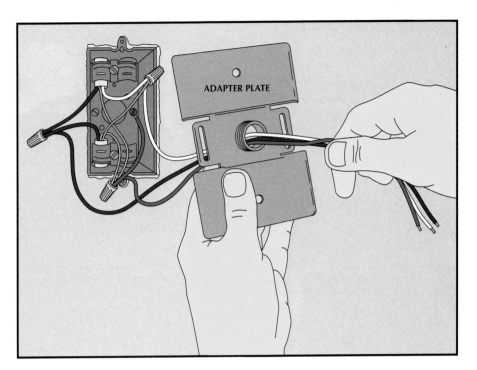

# EXTENDING THE CIRCUIT

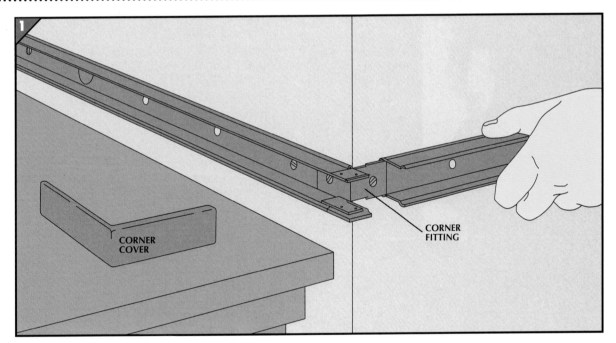

### 1. Turning a corner.

◆ Mark level lines on the wall along the route you have chosen for the raceway.

◆ Hold straight lengths of base raceway on the wall with the top edges even with the lines, and mark the screw holes at each end and every 3 feet in between.

◆ Drill a hole for a screw anchor at each mark and fasten the base pieces to the wall with the screws and anchors supplied.

◆ At an outside corner, cut a base piece to fit flush with the edge of the corner.

◆ Slip one end of a corner fitting into this piece and

tighten the fitting screw securely to ensure a good connection between the two pieces. Tighten the second fitting screw.

◆ Slide a straight base piece over the other end of the corner fitting (above) until the end contacts the second fitting screw.

◆ For inside corners and 90-degree turns that route the raceway up or down, install the appropriate fittings in the same way.

◆ When all the bases are installed, lay in the wires and secure them with wire clips. Do not connect the wires to the power source yet.

## 2. Installing a receptacle.

◆ At each receptacle location along the wire run, strip $\frac{1}{2}$ inch of insulation *(page 19)* from the black and white wires—without cutting the wires—then form the stripped sections into loops, wrap them beneath the terminal screws of a raceway receptacle, and tighten the screws.

◆ Cut the green ground wire, strip the cut ends, and connect the ground wire of the receptacle to the cut ends with a wire cap *(right)*.

◆ Snap the receptacle into the raceway base with the ground wire down.

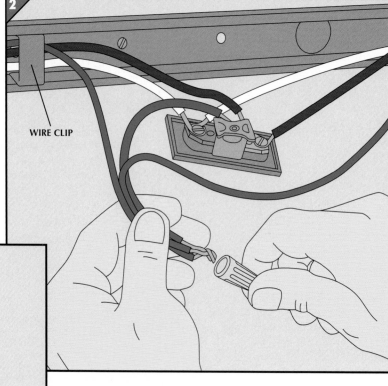

WIRE CLIP

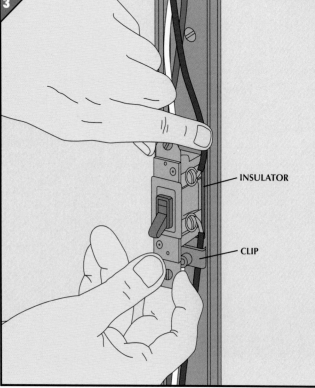

INSULATOR

CLIP

## 3. Installing a switch.

◆ At each switch locaton, cut the black wire and connect the cut ends to the brass switch terminals.

◆ Snap the insulator base supplied with the switch into the raceway base and push the switch into position *(left)*.

◆ Screw the switch to the support clips.

⚠ **CAUTION** *When you push the switch into position, make sure the white and green wires run freely behind the switch, and that the switch does not nick the wires' insulation.*

## 4. Wiring to the power source.

◆ At an outlet box, strip $\frac{1}{2}$ inch of insulation from the ends of the raceway wires and connect the black and white wires to the circuit wires with the pressure-type connectors supplied: black to black and white to white, pushing the wire ends into the holes in the connectors *(right)*. Stagger the location of the connectors so they do not jam the base of the raceway.

◆ Connect the box and raceway ground wires with a wire cap.

◆ Test the new circuit with a voltage tester *(pages 45-47)*, then tuck all wires inside the channels and snap on the raceway covers.

At a service panel, run the raceway wires through the offset connector and nipple, then strip off their ends and connect them to the service panel *(pages 39-40)*. Snap the offset connector cover *(page 26)* over its base.

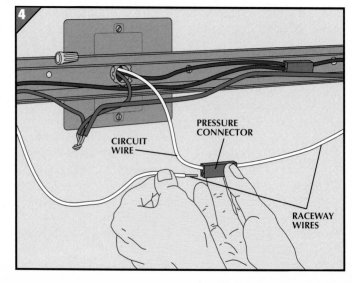

CIRCUIT WIRE

PRESSURE CONNECTOR

RACEWAY WIRES

## 1. Installing the base.

◆ Place the base plate of a raceway floor-outlet box in the desired location, then lay out raceway and fittings on the floor and slide the plate over the end of the raceway *(right)*.

◆ Cut the raceway to the correct length, drill holes in the floor for screw anchors, then fasten the raceway and base plate to the floor.

◆ Lay the wires inside the raceway, secure them with wire clips *(page 27, Step 1)*, then wire the receptacle *(page 28, Step 2)*.

◆ Fasten the receptacle to the base-plate supports.

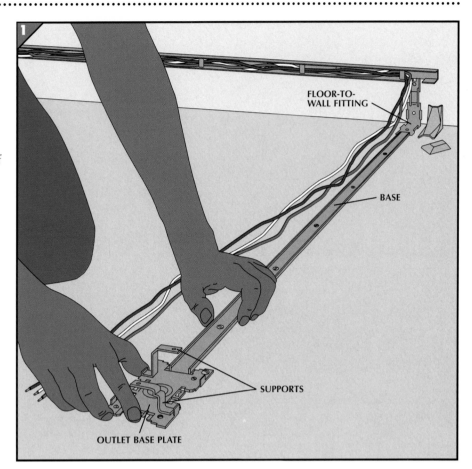

FLOOR-TO-WALL FITTING

BASE

SUPPORTS

OUTLET BASE PLATE

### TRICKS OF THE TRADE

### Covering Power Cords

If you plan to use a mid-floor outlet only rarely, you can forgo installing floor raceway and simply use a power cord plugged into a wall outlet. But cords lying loosely on the floor present a hazard. Protect them temporarily with wood bridges cut from 1-by-3s. Rout a groove along the length of one side of the board to house the cord. Cut bevels on the opposite face so the cover will not be an obstruction when the flat side is against the floor. When the power cord is not in use, remove the wood bridges and unplug the cord.

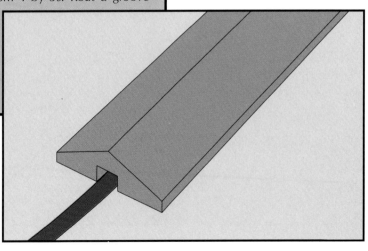

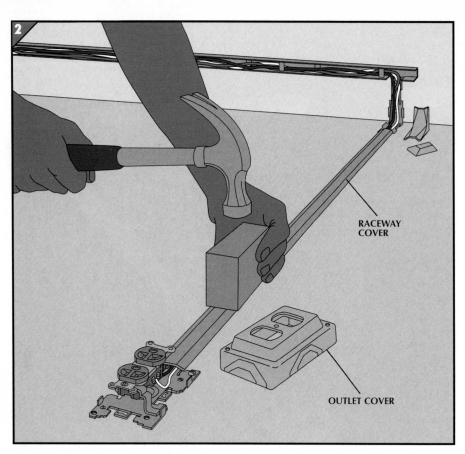

## 2. Securing the cover.

◆ Cut a length of floor-raceway cover to fit between the floor-to-wall fitting and the receptacle base plate.

◆ Force the cover into position by laying one edge along the raceway base and pounding the other side down with a hammer and a wood block *(left)*.

◆ With a pair of pliers, remove the scored semicircle from the outlet cover to fit the end of the raceway cover, then screw the outlet cover to its base.

◆ Install the floor-to-wall fitting cover.

RACEWAY COVER

OUTLET COVER

# RACEWAY FOR BASEBOARD OUTLETS

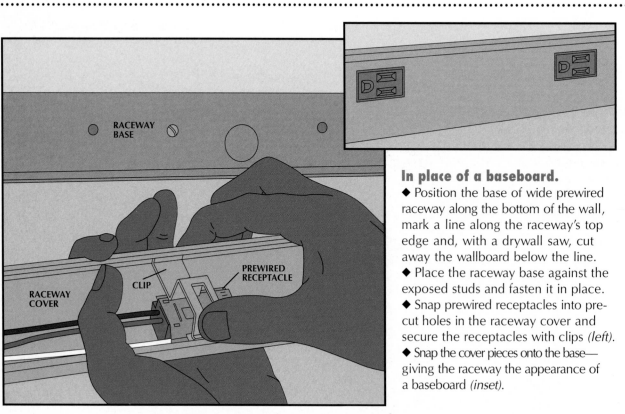

RACEWAY BASE

PREWIRED RECEPTACLE

CLIP

RACEWAY COVER

## In place of a baseboard.

◆ Position the base of wide prewired raceway along the bottom of the wall, mark a line along the raceway's top edge and, with a drywall saw, cut away the wallboard below the line.

◆ Place the raceway base against the exposed studs and fasten it in place.

◆ Snap prewired receptacles into precut holes in the raceway cover and secure the receptacles with clips *(left)*.

◆ Snap the cover pieces onto the base—giving the raceway the appearance of a baseboard *(inset)*.

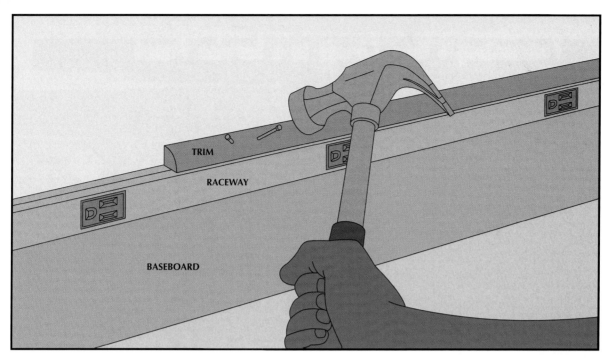

## As part of a baseboard assembly.

◆ Fasten the base of a narrow prewired raceway against a wall along the top of a flat-topped baseboard.
◆ Lay in the wires and snap on the raceway covers.
◆ Cut lengths of quarter-round molding to fit along

the raceway, apply a bead of wood glue to the back of the trim, and fasten it to the wall directly above the raceway with $1\frac{1}{2}$-inch finishing nails *(above)*. Drive two nails every 16 inches through the molding and into the wallboard at crossing angles.

# QUICK CIRCUIT CHANGES

### Removing raceway covers.
◆ To access the wires of an existing raceway, first turn off the power to it.
◆ For floor raceway, remove the cover of a receptacle box *(page 29)*, disconnect the receptacle, and put it aside.
◆ With a screwdriver, pry up one end of the raceway cover while working a pry bar between the floor and the edge of the cover *(right)*.
◆ Work along the raceway with the bar, lifting the pried edge at short intervals.

For a wall raceway, use two screwdrivers to pry the cover from the wall *(inset)*.

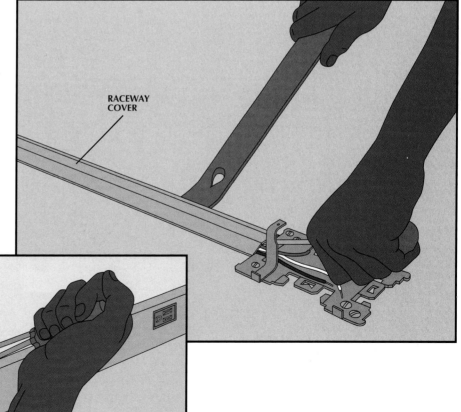

Connecting new cables at the service panel is the final step in installing a new branch circuit. Start by identifying the type of panel box you have and familiarizing yourself with its components. Three common types are shown opposite and on pages 34 and 35, with their doors and safety cover plates removed. If your panel is configured differently from those shown, study its wiring schematic before working on it.

**The Service Panel:** All panels contain metal assemblies called bus bars or buses, which conduct electricity within the panel, and a number of circuit breakers or fuses that protect the house wiring against short circuits and overloads. Two power buses conduct current from the "hot" wires of the 240-volt main feeder cable to the fuses or breakers, which pass it on to individual circuits. The metal conductor strips that carry current in these buses are generally hidden behind the fuses or breakers. A ground/neutral bar connects the neutral wire of the feeder cable to the terminals for the neutral and ground leads of the branch circuits.

**Adding Circuits:** A 240-volt branch circuit draws power from both power buses, a 120-volt circuit from only one bus. It is important that the loads on the two power buses be balanced as evenly as possible; when you hook up a new branch circuit, choose a breaker or fuse position fed by the bus that bears the lighter load *(page 125)*. Your panel may have one of two basic power-bus patterns: straight bus *(opposite and page 34)* and split bus *(page 35)*.

Branch circuits can be added to a panel only if it has vacant positions for breakers or fuses and a total amperage that can handle the additional load *(pages 122-125)*. If you have a fuse panel with no vacant positions, install a subpanel *(pages 41-44)* or replace the main one *(pages 50-56)*. In some cases "piggyback" or "skinny" breakers can be used *(page 40)*.

>
> ⚠ *If your system has aluminum wiring,*
> **CAUTION** *have a specially trained, licensed electrician install the new circuit.*

> ⚠ *Always shut off power upstream of the service panel (pages 62-65)*
> **CAUTION** *before removing the cover plate, and do not restore power until you have tested the new circuits and their outlets (pages 45-47). Unplug large appliances, then plug them back in one at a time to avoid overloading the system.*

**TOOLS**

Screwdriver
Solenoid voltage tester
Hammer
Pliers
Nail set
Cable ripper
Multipurpose tool

**MATERIALS**

Knockout filler plate
Electrical cable
Cable clamps
Fuse adapters
Plug fuses
Skinny circuit breakers
Piggyback circuit breakers

## FUSES AND BREAKERS

In a circuit-breaker panel, single-pole breakers, making contact with a single power bus, protect the 120-volt branch circuits. Double-pole breakers, spanning both buses, serve the 240-volt circuits. An overload will cause a breaker to switch the power off; when the overload has been corrected, the breaker can be reset by flipping the switch back to "On."

A fuse box generally contains two different types of fuses. Plug fuses, which screw into sockets, protect 120-volt circuits carrying 30 amperes or less. Cartridge fuses, installed in pullouts that resemble small drawers, protect 240-volt circuits carrying large currents. Both types work in the same way: When a circuit is overloaded, a metal strip in the fuse melts, cutting off power to the circuit. When the cause of the overload has been found and corrected, a new fuse must be installed.

In a fully wired breaker panel, "piggyback" or "skinny" breakers can be used to make room for two branch circuits in one bus opening—provided the panel's amperage can handle the total load. A piggyback—technically called a tandem breaker—is the same size as a normal breaker, but it contains two circuit breakers in a single plastic case. A skinny—technically called a half-module breaker—resembles a normal breaker but is only half as wide so that two can fit in a normal opening.

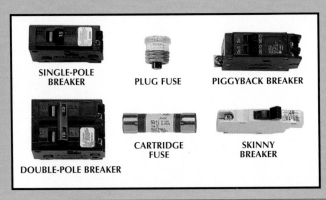

SINGLE-POLE BREAKER    PLUG FUSE    PIGGYBACK BREAKER

DOUBLE-POLE BREAKER    CARTRIDGE FUSE    SKINNY BREAKER

**A circuit-breaker panel.**
This circuit-breaker panel is powered by a 240-volt service cable. The braided neutral lead of the cable connects to the main neutral lug—a type of setscrew pressure connector—and is linked to the branch-circuit neutral and ground wires at the ground/neutral bar. The service cable's hot leads enter a double-pole main breaker, whose two switches control the two 120-volt power buses that pass down the back of the panel beneath breakers of smaller amperages. Turning off the main breaker cuts off power to all the smaller breakers, and in turn, to the entire house. The smaller breakers serve to interrupt power to branch circuits should any circuit become overloaded.

A double-pole circuit breaker, connected to both the A and B power buses, protects a 240-volt circuit. Single-pole circuit breakers that protect the 120-volt branch circuits are connected alternately to the power buses in an A-B-A-B pattern. The branch-circuit cables enter the panel through knockouts and are secured to the box with cable clamps; their neutral and ground leads are fastened to the setscrews of the ground/neutral bar, while the hot leads are attached to the branch-circuit setscrews next to the breakers.

Split-bus circuit-breaker panels, similar to the split-bus fuse panel on page 35, are common in houses built before 1981. These panels do not have a single main circuit breaker. Up to six separate high-amp breakers must be switched off to interrupt power

throughout the house. If you have such a panel, it is best to replace it with a straight-bus type before you expand or upgrade your house wiring (*pages 50-56*).

Service-panel equipment produced by different manufacturers is rarely interchangeable. When purchasing new circuit breakers, note the make and model number of the service panel to make sure that the new breakers will fit it.

⚠️ **CAUTION** *Throwing the main breaker on a straight-bus panel, or up to six breakers in a split-bus panel, will turn off power throughout the house, but will not completely kill the power in the service panel. Only by shutting off power at the meter (page 65) or at the main disconnect (pages 62-64) can the panel be made safe to work on.*

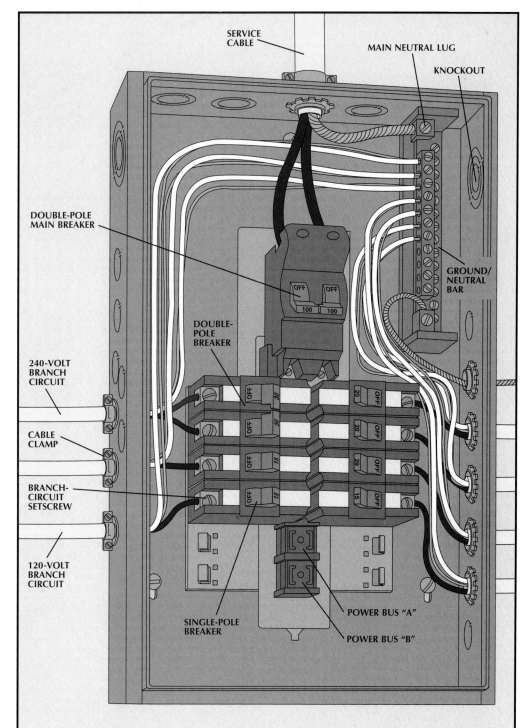

SERVICE CABLE

MAIN NEUTRAL LUG

KNOCKOUT

DOUBLE-POLE MAIN BREAKER

240-VOLT BRANCH CIRCUIT

CABLE CLAMP

BRANCH-CIRCUIT SETSCREW

120-VOLT BRANCH CIRCUIT

DOUBLE-POLE BREAKER

GROUND/NEUTRAL BAR

OFF 100 100

OFF 30 20 OFF

OFF 30 20 OFF

OFF 15 20 OFF

OFF 15 15 OFF

SINGLE-POLE BREAKER

POWER BUS "A"

POWER BUS "B"

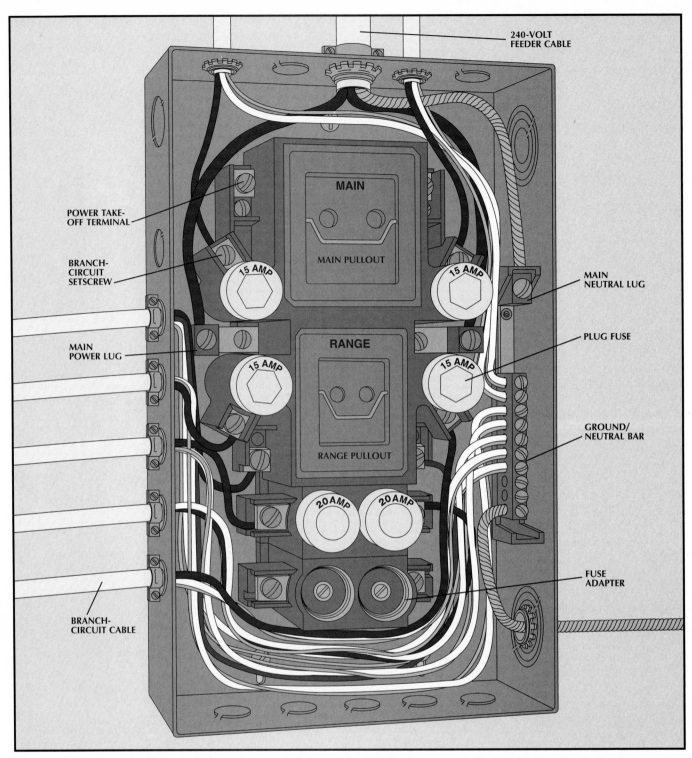

240-VOLT
FEEDER CABLE

POWER TAKE-
OFF TERMINAL

BRANCH-
CIRCUIT
SETSCREW

MAIN
POWER LUG

BRANCH-
CIRCUIT CABLE

MAIN

MAIN PULLOUT

15 AMP

15 AMP

RANGE

RANGE PULLOUT

15 AMP

15 AMP

20 AMP

20 AMP

MAIN
NEUTRAL LUG

PLUG FUSE

GROUND/
NEUTRAL BAR

FUSE
ADAPTER

## A straight-bus fuse panel.

A 240-volt feeder cable enters this panel box at the top. The two power leads of the cable are attached to the main power lugs, which are linked to the fuse receptacles by two 120-volt power buses—vertical metal bars, hidden behind the devices in the center of the panel. A single main pullout can be removed to turn off the power to all the fuses; a smaller pullout beneath protects a 120/240-volt branch circuit that feeds a large appliance such as an electric range. The pullout contains two cartridge fuses that snap into metal spring-clip contacts. Plug fuses ranging up to 30 amperes protect six 120-volt circuits. The fuses at right conduct cur-

rent from one bus; the fuses at left, from the other. Two power takeoff terminals at the top of the panel could provide wiring for a subpanel. While the terminals of the empty fuses could serve more branch circuits, fuse adapters, required by code in most localities, are permanent devices screwed into the panel to prevent high-amperage fuses from being placed in low-amperage circuits (page 39, Step 2).

Adding a new 240-volt branch circuit to a straight-bus fuse panel may be impossible: Many such panels have two or three 240-volt positions, and every available position may already be filled. In this case, add a subpanel (pages 41-44), or replace the main panel with a larger circuit-breaker panel (pages 50-56).

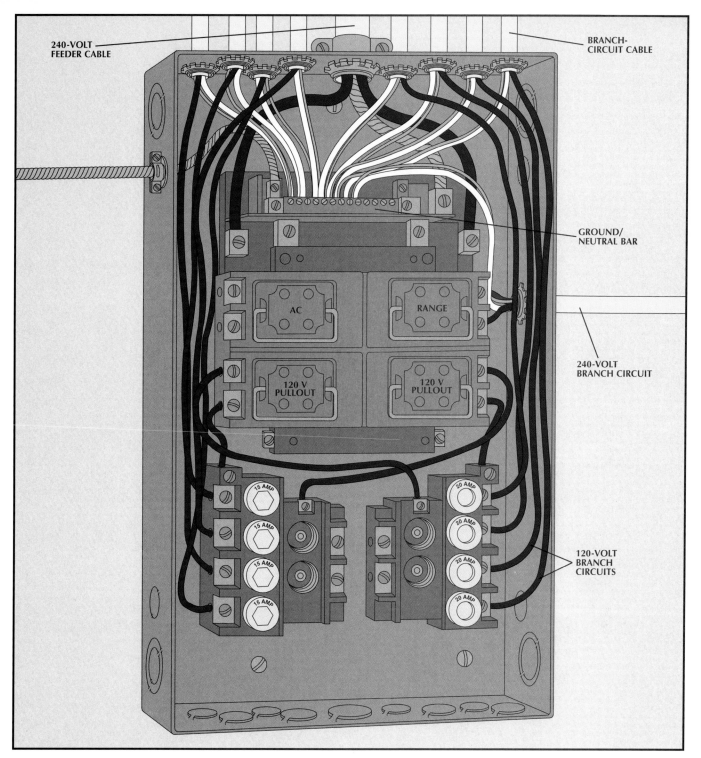

240-VOLT FEEDER CABLE

BRANCH-CIRCUIT CABLE

GROUND/ NEUTRAL BAR

AC

RANGE

120 V PULLOUT

120 V PULLOUT

240-VOLT BRANCH CIRCUIT

15 AMP
15 AMP
15 AMP
15 AMP

20 AMP
20 AMP
20 AMP
20 AMP

120-VOLT BRANCH CIRCUITS

## The split-bus fuse panel.

No single main pullout in this panel will shut all the power off; current flows through divided buses, and all four pullouts must be removed to cut off all the power in the house. The service cable goes to two power buses behind the pullouts, split into sections, each connected to an individual pullout. Plug fuses for the 120-volt branch circuits are protected by two pullouts. The remaining pullouts serve 240-volt circuits for such appliances as the range or air conditioner. The pullouts contain cartridge fuses, which are rated up to 60 amps.

If you are planning to upgrade your system and you have a split-bus panel, first replace it with a circuit-breaker type *(pages 50-56).*

# THE BASIC SAFETY TEST

## Checking a circuit-breaker panel.

◆ Before working on the panel, switch off power at the main breakers, then shut off power at the meter *(page 65)* or at the main disconnect *(pages 62-64)*.

◆ Ground one prong of a solenoid voltage tester on the ground/neutral bar and touch the other prong firmly to each of the hot supply lugs near the main shutoff. If the tester registers any indication of voltage, stop work immediately and call an electrician to shut off power and inspect the connections in the panel.

◆ As insurance, also test the branch circuits, touching the prongs of the tester to the ground/neutral bar and to each of the two power buses in the center of the panel *(right)*; snap out adjoining single-pole breakers to access the buses, if necessary.

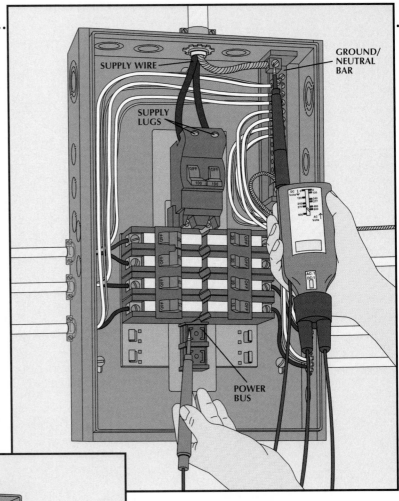

## Checking a fuse panel.

◆ Before working on the panel, switch off power at the main fuses, then shut off power at the meter *(page 65)* or at the main disconnect *(pages 62-64)*.

◆ Ground one prong of a solenoid voltage tester on the ground/neutral bar and touch the other prong firmly to each of the hot supply lugs near the main shutoff. If the tester registers any indication of voltage, stop work immediately and call an electrician to shut off power and inspect the connections in the panel.

◆ As insurance, also test the branch circuits, touching the prongs of the tester to the ground/neutral bar and to each of the branch-circuit setscrews *(left)*.

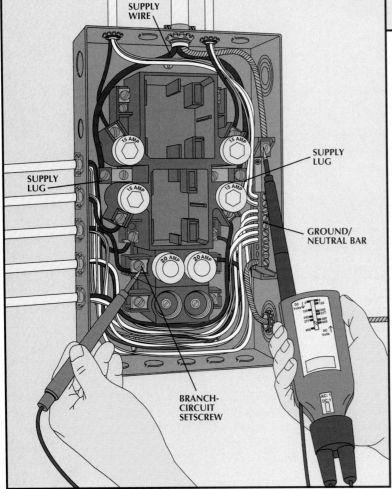

# REMOVING A PANEL KNOCKOUT

### 1. Punching out the center.

To add cables for branch circuits, you will first need to remove knockouts on the sides, top, or bottom of the service-panel box.

◆ On the central section of a multi-section knockout, place the tip of a nail set opposite the tie to the first knockout ring, and tap the knockout center inward with a hammer *(right)*.

◆ Grip the center from inside the box with a pair of pliers and work it free. Removing the center is sufficient for cables smaller than No. 10. For larger cables, remove one or more rings from the knockout *(Steps 2 and 3)*.

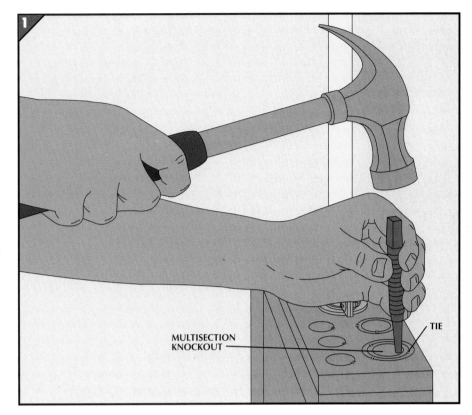

MULTISECTION KNOCKOUT

TIE

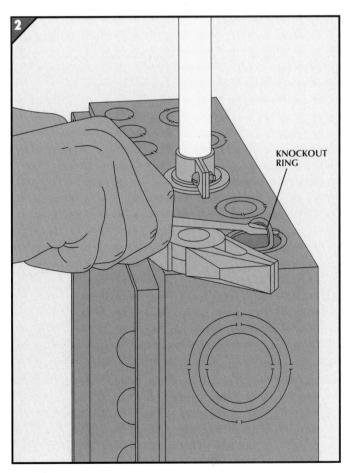

KNOCKOUT RING

### 2. Prying up a ring.

◆ Set the tip of a screwdriver midway between the knockout ring's ties and pry up one side of the ring. To make this step easier, lever the screwdriver with a pair of pliers set flat against the box *(left)*.

◆ Pry up the other side of the ring in the same way.

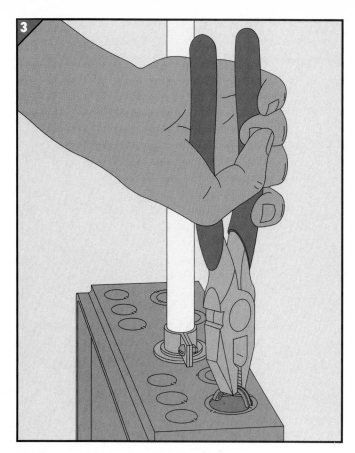

### 3. Removing the ring.
◆ Grasp both sides of the knockout ring with pliers *(left)* and work the ring free.
◆ To enlarge the hole further, remove additional rings by prying them in or out with a screwdriver, then working them free with pliers.

# CLOSING A HOLE IN THE BOX

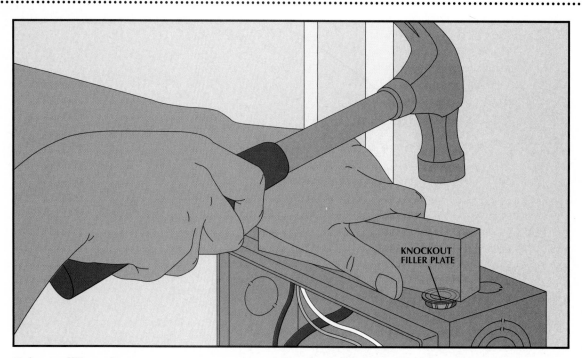

KNOCKOUT FILLER PLATE

### Using a filler plate.
According to code regulations, you must seal any unused knockout holes. To do so, place a knockout filler plate, available at electrical-supply stores, into the hole and tap it into place with a wood block and a hammer *(above)*.

# WIRING A NEW CIRCUIT TO A FUSE PANEL

## 1. Making the connections.

◆ Shut off power at the meter *(page 65)* or at the main disconnect *(pages 62-64)*. Then, run the new circuit cable through a knockout hole and fasten it to the panel with a cable clamp, drawing the cables far enough into the box to provide slack for tucking the wires out of the way.

◆ Outside the box, label the cable with a marked piece of masking tape indicating its amperage, voltage, and function. Inside the box, strip the cable and its wires *(pages 18-19)*.

◆ For a 120-volt circuit, attach the white neutral lead to the ground/neutral bar, the green or bare copper ground lead to the same terminal in the bar, and the black lead to an unused branch circuit setscrew *(right)*. For a 120/240-volt circuit, attach the white/neutral lead and the green or copper ground lead to the same terminal in the ground/neutral bar, and the red and black leads to the two setscrews of an unused pullout.

> ⚠️ **CAUTION** *Never attach the red and black leads of a 120/240-volt circuit to two 120-volt setscrews.*

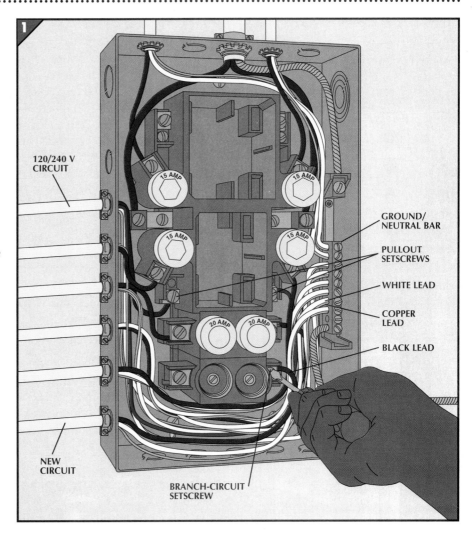

120/240 V CIRCUIT

GROUND/ NEUTRAL BAR

PULLOUT SETSCREWS

WHITE LEAD

COPPER LEAD

BLACK LEAD

NEW CIRCUIT

BRANCH-CIRCUIT SETSCREW

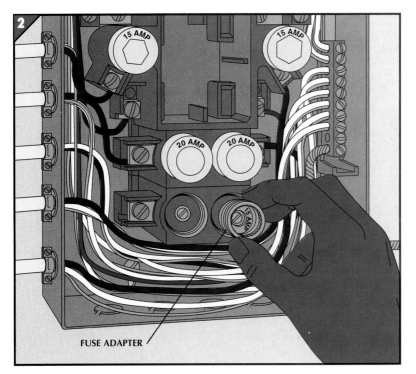

FUSE ADAPTER

## 2. Installing a fuse adapter.

To be sure that you will protect the new branch circuit with a fuse of the correct rating, screw a fuse adapter with the same amperage as the circuit into the fuse receptacle *(left)*.

> ⚠️ **CAUTION** *Check the ampere rating of the adapter carefully before you screw it in; the device has a spring-loaded barb that prevents it from being removed after installation.*

# INSTALLING A SPACESAVING BREAKER

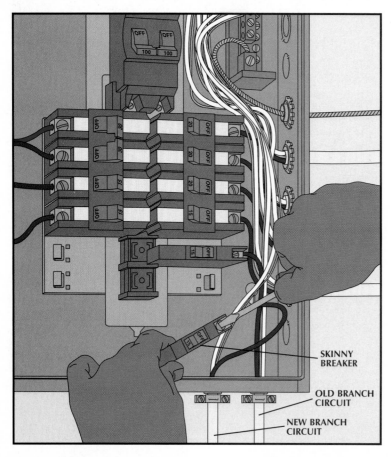

SKINNY BREAKER

OLD BRANCH CIRCUIT

NEW BRANCH CIRCUIT

## Attaching wires to skinny breakers.

◆ Shut off power at the meter *(page 65)* or at the main disconnect *(pages 62-64)*.

◆ Run the new circuit cable into the box, and strip the cable and wires as for a fuse panel *(pages 18-19)*. If there is no room in the box for an additional circuit breaker, you can replace an existing one with a pair of skinnies as shown at left or a piggyback *(below)* of the same amperage as the removed breaker.

◆ Attach the neutral and ground wires of the new circuit to the ground/neutral bar in the box.

◆ Switch a single-pole breaker to "Off," remove it from the service panel, and unhook the black lead attached to it.

◆ Wire this black lead to a skinny breaker *(left)* and snap the breaker into the box.

◆ Attach the black lead of the new branch circuit to a second skinny and install it alongside the first.

⚠ **CAUTION** *Purchase a breaker that is compatible with your model of service panel; never force a breaker into a panel for which it is not designed. Never wire the hot leads of 240-volt branch circuit to a skinny breaker; the breaker fills a position on only one power bus and is restricted to 120-volt circuits.*

## Installing a piggyback breaker.

◆ Shut off power at the meter *(page 65)* or at the main disconnect *(pages 62-64)*.

◆ Wire a piggyback breaker as you would a pair of skinnies, as described above, but attach the black lead from the removed breaker to one of the terminals at the base of the piggyback, and the black lead of the new branch circuit to the piggyback's second terminal.

◆ Snap the piggyback into the panel box *(right)*.

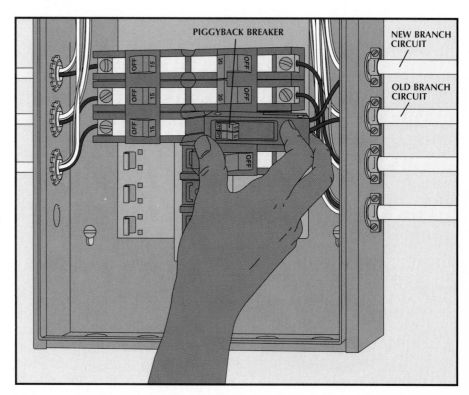

PIGGYBACK BREAKER

NEW BRANCH CIRCUIT

OLD BRANCH CIRCUIT

# The Flexibility of a Subpanel

When you want to add branch circuits to your electrical system, it is often best to feed them through a new subpanel—a scaled-down version of a service panel—instead of connecting them directly to the main panel.

**Advantages of a Subpanel:** The principal use of a subpanel is to add circuits to a main panel equipped with fuses, since a fuse box rarely has room for additional fuses. The solution is a new subpanel mounted near the old fuse box to protect the added circuits. But a subpanel can also be placed in a location that makes wiring distant branch circuits easier. Instead of snaking every branch circuit back to the main panel, you need to run only one high-capacity feeder cable between the main panel and the subpanel.

**Calculating Loads:** Before you install a subpanel, calculate the total load it will carry and make sure that the main panel will not be overloaded by the new circuits you plan to add; if it will be, have the electric company increase the service to your house so you can install a new panel *(pages 50-56)*. Determine the size of the subpanel and the feeder cable by calculating the amperage of the branch circuits you plan to connect *(pages 124-125)*.

A typical subpanel is fed with 240 volts from the main panel by SER cable and contains breaker positions for two to six branch circuits. If all you have is 120-volt service at the main panel, you may be able to add a subpanel to it, but it is generally preferable to replace a 120-volt main panel with a 120/240-volt circuit-breaker panel of ample capacity. In some localities, codes prohibit the addition of subpanels to 120-volt main panels.

**Making the Connections:** Before installing the subpanel, run the branch-circuit cables and the feeder cable to the subpanel location, arranging them so that all enter the box from one side. Then connect the cables to the subpanel terminals and test the installation. Check the local code to determine whether the new subpanel must be approved by an electrical inspector before you attach the feeder to the main panel.

 *Always shut off power at the meter (page 65) or at the* **CAUTION** *main disconnect (pages 62-64) before working on the panel. If your system has aluminum wiring (page 11), have a specially trained, licensed electrician install the subpanel.*

 *When cutting into walls or ceilings, always take pre-* **CAUTION** *cautions against releasing lead and asbestos particles into the air (page 12).*

---

**T TOOLS**

Screwdriver
Hammer
Nail set
Pliers

Electric drill
Spade bit
Keyhole saw
Continuity tester
Solenoid voltage
  tester

**M MATERIALS**

Subpanel
SER cable
Branch-circuit cable
Cable clamps

Ground bus bar
Circuit breakers
Round-head wood
  screws (1" No. 8)
Wire caps
Jumper wire

**SAFETY TIPS**

*Put on goggles before operating a power tool.*

---

## 1. Mounting the ground bus bar.

◆ Buy a ground bus bar that is appropriate for the type and model of subpanel you are installing.
◆ Holding the bar where it will not interfere with the knockouts you will use, and aligning its mounting holes over two pretapped holes in the back of the box, fasten the bar with the screws provided *(right)*. If the panel has no holes, make them with a drill.
◆ Remove knockouts along one side of the box *(pages 37-38)*.

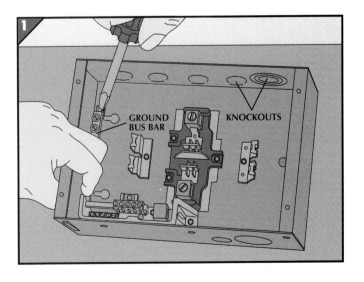

GROUND BUS BAR

KNOCKOUTS

## 2. Mounting the box.

◆ To flush-mount the box, cut a hole in the wall for the subpanel box *(page 15, Step 1)*, aligning the edge that will run along the mounting side of the box with the face of a stud.

◆ Pull the branch-circuit and feeder cables through separate knockouts and secure them with cable clamps.

◆ Push the box into the wall, wired side first *(right)*, so that its front edges are flush with the surface of the wall.

◆ Fasten the mounting side of the box flush against the stud with 1-inch round-head No. 8 wood screws.

For a surface mount, attach the subpanel to plywood *(page 53, Step 2)*, then pull in the wires and secure the clamps.

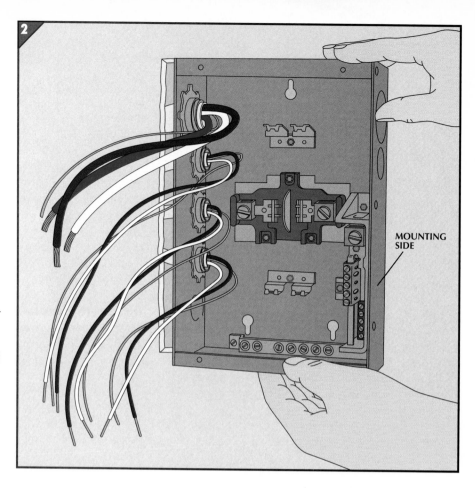

MOUNTING SIDE

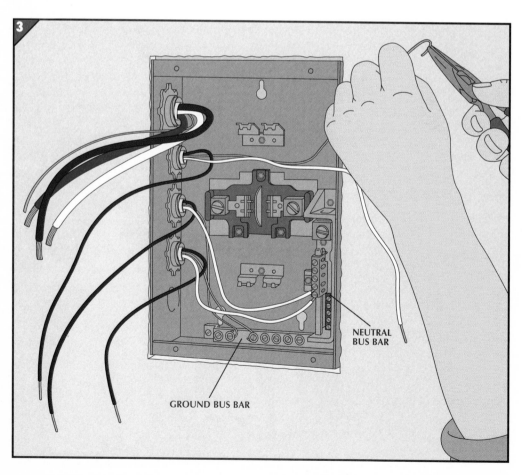

NEUTRAL BUS BAR

GROUND BUS BAR

## 3. Wiring the circuits.

◆ Test the unconnected branch circuits *(pages 45-47)*.

◆ Working on one circuit at a time, use pliers to form a hook in the stripped end of each green or copper ground wire *(left)* and connect the wire to the ground bus bar.

◆ Connect each white neutral wire to the neutral bus bar.

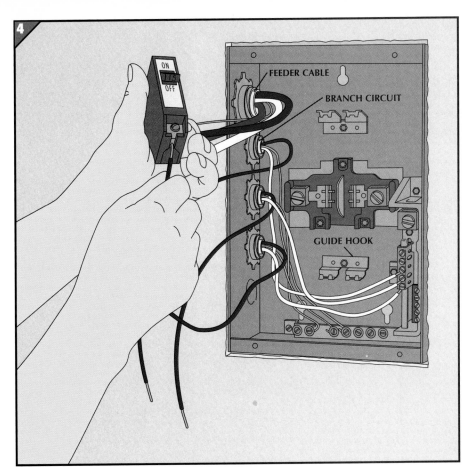

## 4. Wiring the circuit breakers.

◆ Push the black lead of each 120-volt branch circuit into the terminal at the bottom front of a single-pole breaker of the proper amperage *(left)*, and tighten the setscrew.

◆ Slip the breaker over its guide hook in the panel box and snap the breaker down to lock it into place.

◆ If you are wiring a 240-volt branch circuit, install a double-pole breaker in the same way, inserting both the black and red leads into its terminals.

## 5. Connecting the feeder cable.

◆ Attach the feeder cable's bare copper or green insulated wire to the ground bus bar as in Step 3.

◆ Insert the stripped end of the white feeder wire into the neutral lug at one end of the neutral bus bar *(right)* and tighten the setscrew.

◆ Attach the black and red conductors to the subpanel power terminals in the same way.

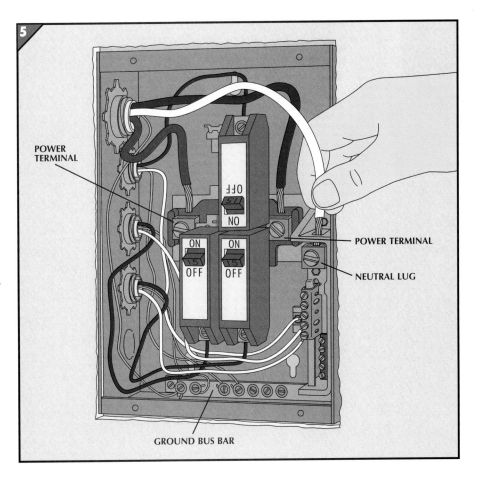

## 6. Wiring the feeder to the service panel.

◆ Shut off power at the meter *(page 65)* or at the main disconnect *(pages 62-64)* before working on the panel, and check that the panel is dead *(page 36)*.

◆ For a circuit-breaker panel, connect the feeder-cable wires as you would a 240-volt branch circuit *(page 56, Step 2)*.

◆ In a fuse box, remove the pullouts and attach the feeder-cable ground wire to an unused terminal on the branch-circuit ground bus bar.

◆ Attach the feeder neutral conductor to the neutral lug *(right)*.

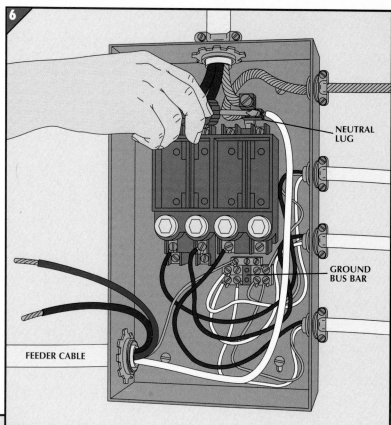

NEUTRAL LUG

GROUND BUS BAR

FEEDER CABLE

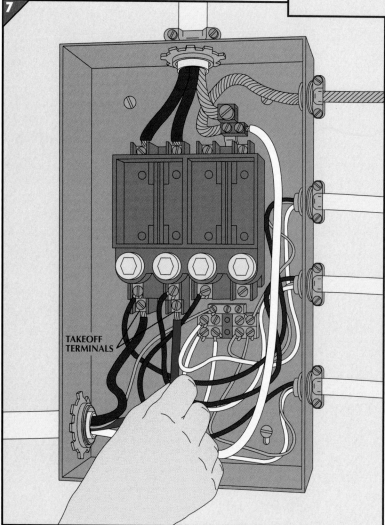

TAKEOFF TERMINALS

## 7. Connecting the power leads.

◆ Insert either the red or black feeder lead into a takeoff terminal and tighten the setscrew. Attach the remaining lead to the other terminal in the same way *(left)*.

◆ Install the pullouts you removed in Step 6.

◆ With either a fuse box or a circuit-breaker panel, replace the safety cover on the subpanel.

◆ Restore power and test the new branch circuits *(opposite)*.

**F**ew things are more frustrating than errors made in wiring a circuit. Locating flaws can be uncertain, mystifying, and—occasionally—dangerous. Nevertheless, electricians have worked out a set of procedures that usually finds the problem quickly and safely.

**Common Problems:** The trouble almost always takes one of two forms: short circuits that disable the new circuit, and wiring mistakes that make it unsafe or prevent it from functioning properly.

A short circuit is a fault that causes a direct connection from a hot wire to either a neutral wire or the ground (and in 240-volt circuits from one hot wire to the other). Test for shorts before you connect the circuit at the service panel. Separate and tape the stripped ends of hot and neutral wires at the panel and turn all switches to "On"; do not screw light bulbs into sockets or plug appliances into receptacles. Then go to the outlet at the end

of the run and hook a continuity tester *(page 8)* across each possible combination of hot wires, connecting each to other hot wires, to neutral wires, and to ground. If the bulb glows, the circuit is shorted. Also test each neutral wire to ground; a glow indicates a grounded neutral wire that must be repaired. To find the cause of trouble, look for the clues shown on page 46— which also serve for troubleshooting short circuits in existing wiring *(box, below)*. When you have repaired the wiring fault, you can connect the circuit at the panel with the assurance that it will not blow fuses or trip circuit breakers, and can go on to test the circuit for mistakes that can be discovered only with the current on.

**Testing Tools:** Normally, wiring mistakes occur at receptacles, and can be diagnosed with two inexpensive tools: a receptacle analyzer and a solenoid voltage tester *(pages 8 and 47)*. Of the five mistakes that can be detected by the analyzer, one is of particular

concern. If hot and neutral wires are reversed at the receptacle terminals, a serious hazard is introduced, for with such appliances as CD players, radios, refrigerators, and television sets, their polarized plugs (three-pronged plugs and plugs with two prongs of different widths) may send current to their metal cabinets.

Two other kinds of miswiring detectable by the analyzer can energize the outlet box in which a receptacle is mounted: reversed hot and ground wires, and a combination of a disconnected ground wire and a hot wire shorted to the box.

Though these tests are made at outlets alone, they are likely to answer your purposes. But finding problems in circuits can be tricky, and a mistake in diagnosis very serious. Even if you locate one wiring error there may be another; always retest. Unless you are absolutely certain you have located all of the defects, and always if you suspect the defect is in a run of cable, call an electrician.

 **TOOLS**    Screwdriver     Receptacle analyzer       **MATERIALS**   Wire caps
                 Continuity tester    Solenoid voltage tester                           Jumper wire

## WHAT TO DO WHEN BREAKERS KEEP TRIPPING OR FUSES KEEP BLOWING

When a breaker trips or a fuse blows, the fault is either an overload or a short circuit. Check for overloading, the most common cause, by adding up the amperages on the circuit, allowing for the starting draw of motors and fluorescent lights *(pages 124-125)*. Correct overloading temporarily by unplugging a few of the appliances, and permanently by installing a new branch circuit *(pages 32-40)*.

In a circuit that is not overloaded, search for a short. Unplug appliances from all dead outlets and turn switches that control inoperative fixtures to "On." Reset the breaker or replace the fuse. If the breaker does not trip or the fuse blow, the short is in one appliance. You may find it by inspecting the appliance plugs for strands of wire between the prongs, and their cords for fraying or bare spots. Failing that, have the appliance repaired as necessary.

Shorts within the circuit itself are rare but possible. Wires heat up slightly when current flows through them, then cool off when the current stops; the corresponding cycle of expansion and contraction can dry and crack the insulation or break a nicked wire. Elsewhere, wires can even break from constant slight bending or vibration.

Troubleshoot an existing circuit for shorts as you would a new circuit. Shut off power at the meter *(page 65)* or at the main disconnect *(pages 62-64)* and unhook the circuit at the panel. Missing insulation or a black burn spot where a hot wire has sparked against a grounded outlet box may indicate a short. Even if you find a clear case of one, search the boxes on the circuit for others. If you cannot be sure that you have found and repaired the defect, or if it appears to be in the cables, have an electrician find the trouble.

# THREE COMMON CAUSES OF SHORTS

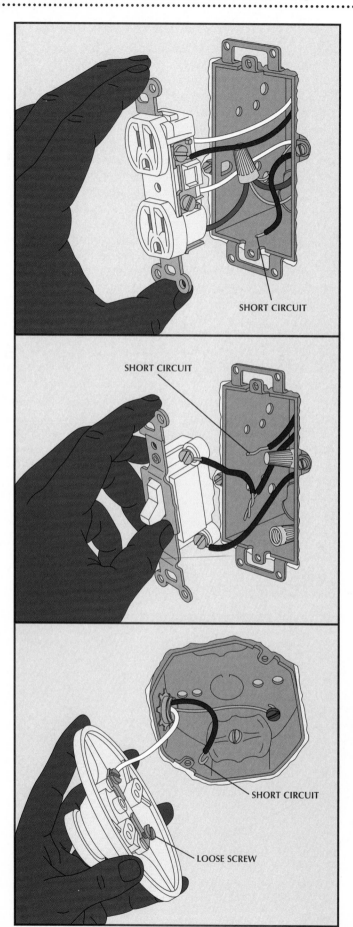

SHORT CIRCUIT

SHORT CIRCUIT

SHORT CIRCUIT

LOOSE SCREW

## Recognizing the basic clues.

Make sure power to the circuit is off at the service panel and, one by one, pull receptacles, switches, and fixtures out of the outlet boxes and look for hot wires that have broken free from their terminals and sprung into contact with the box or a ground wire. If you find a broken wire *(top)*, nicked by wire strippers set a size too small, repair the short by reconnecting the sprung wire. If it is too short to reach its terminal, either loosen the cable clamp and pull in some slack, or wire-cap the short wire to a jumper wire about 2 inches long. If a downward-pointing wire cap has fallen off and let a wire spring away *(middle)*, reinstall the cap so it is pointing upward. For a loose terminal screw *(bottom)*, reconnect the loose wire and tighten the screw.

If you do not find any sprung wires, look for overtightened cable clamps that have cut through cable sheathing and wire insulation, or for hot wires that were accidentally bared when the cable sheathing was stripped off. You may be able to make a repair by pulling slack cable into the box and reconnecting the hot wire; if not, replace the run of cable.

When you have made your repairs, screw all receptacles, switches, or fixtures back into place and run another continuity test. When you are certain that all of the shorts have been eliminated, install cover plates on the outlet boxes, screw the light bulbs into the fixtures, and connect any new circuits at the service panel.

# READING A RECEPTACLE

**Analyzing a 120-volt circuit.**

◆ To check outlets, plug a receptacle analyzer into each outlet on a circuit *(right)*.

◆ If the tester's lights do not signal "OK," turn off the circuit and repair the wiring defect that is indicated on the analyzer panel. Correct any reversed wiring by switching the indicated wires; find open connections in the same way you would find a short *(opposite)*.

◆ To check a switch that fails to work, turn off the circuit.

◆ Repair any open connections; then turn the switch to "On" and connect a continuity tester to the switch terminals.

◆ If the tester bulb does not glow, replace the switch.

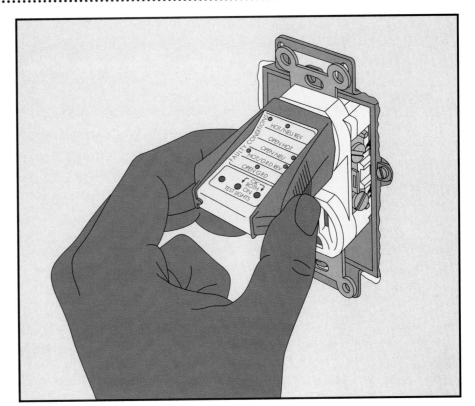

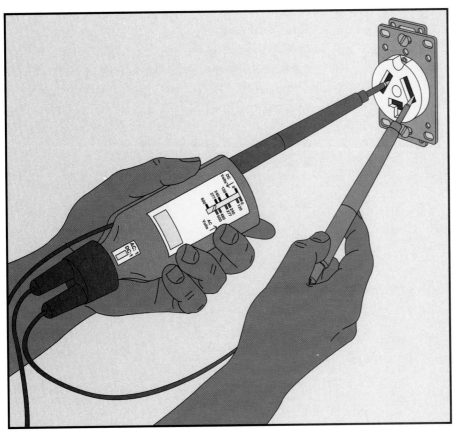

**Testing a 120/240-volt circuit.**

◆ Insert the probes of a solenoid voltage tester into the straight slots of the receptacle *(left)*; the reading should be 240 volts. If not, turn off the circuit and rewire the receptacle with the white wire in the terminal marked "white" and the red and black wires in the other two terminals.

◆ Insert one probe into the L-shaped slot and the other into each of the straight slots in turn; in both cases, the readings should be 120 volts. If not, turn off the circuit and rewire the receptacle.

# 2 Bringing More Current to a House

New circuits and large appliances may demand more power than your meter, panel, and cable provide. To get it, you can put in higher-amperage components that draw more energy from the power company's lines. In the process, you can also improve your electrical system by adding a main disconnect, installing a lightning-surge arrester, or moving the meter to a more suitable location.

Grounding a main disconnect →

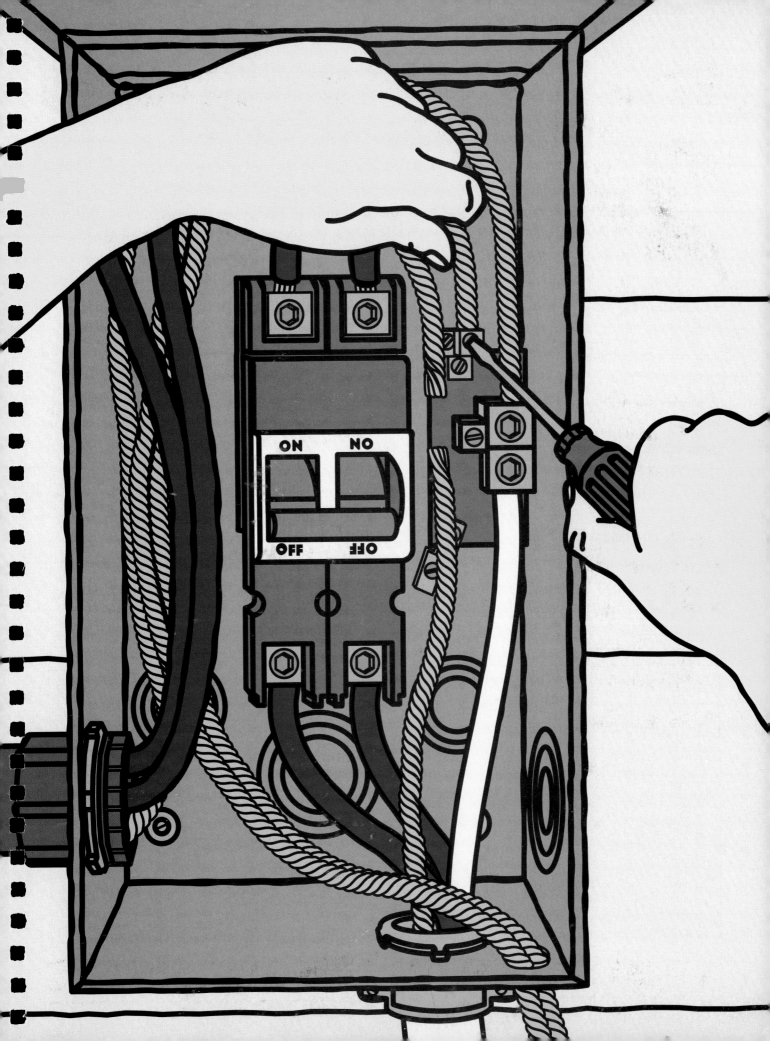

# Replacing the Main Service Panel

New service panels are sometimes installed to provide wiring connections for additional branch circuits or to replace fuses with circuit breakers. More often, though, a new panel upgrades an electrical service to bring in more power.

**Adding Current:** If the main fuse blows or the main circuit breaker trips from time to time, you probably need more power; if you plan to install branch circuits that would overload an existing panel, you certainly do. To get more current, you must install not only a new service panel of greater amperage, but also a meter socket to match *(pages 66-67)*, a new weatherhead or underground connection *(pages 73-81)*, and the cable, conduit, and wire that link these service components.

Before you start, obtain an electrical construction permit—some codes require that a licensed electrician do much or all of this work. Then, contact the power company. A representative will show you where to mount the new meter and panel.

**Installing the Panel:** The service panel is always the first part of the new service to be installed. Unless your house has a separate main disconnect *(pages 62-64)*, you must mount the panel as close as possible to the point where supply wires from the new meter will enter the house. Access to a panel cannot be obstructed; allow at least 3 feet of clear space in front and on either side of the panel and do not place it in a confined or wet location such as a closet or a bathroom. After you

have mounted the new panel and wired its branch circuits and supply cable *(pages 52-56)*, label the branch circuits according to their function *(opposite, Step 1)*.

Make sure that the grounding system meets the requirements described on pages 57 to 59, then make an appointment for an electrical inspection. When your work has been inspected and approved, the electric company will make the final connections to restore service.

> ⚠️ **CAUTION** *Always shut off power at the meter (page 65) or at the main disconnect (pages 62-64) before working on the panel. If your system has aluminum wiring (page 11), have a specially trained, licensed electrician replace the panel.*

 **TOOLS**

Screwdriver
Long-nose pliers
Keyhole saw
Level

Electrician's knife
Diagonal
   cutting pliers
Hex wrench
Wrench
Multipurpose tool

Continuity
   tester
Receptacle
   analyzer
Solenoid
   voltage tester

 **MATERIALS**

Plywood ($\frac{3}{4}$")
Electric panel

Bonding clips
Round-head wood
   screws ($1\frac{1}{2}$" No. 8)
Grounding wire

Cable clamps
Grounding bar
Circuit breakers

---

## Buying Panels and Accessories

✔ Calculate the amount of current you need *(pages 124-125)* to determine what capacity panel you need—100, 125, 150, or 200 amps.

✔ Count the number of circuits you already have—piggybacks *(page 40)* count as two—and buy a panel that has at least six more openings for circuit breakers than you have.

✔ Determine whether you need a weatherproof panel to mount outdoors, or one that is restricted to indoor use.

✔ Decide whether you want a panel with built-in main circuit breakers *(page 33)*, or a separate main disconnect *(pages 55 and 62-65)*. Local electrical code may require special variations—either a separate box that houses a meter and a main disconnect (instead of a disconnect

located at the top of the panel) or a single box that houses both a meter and a service panel.

✔ Choose the mounting style you prefer—flush or surface *(page 53)*.

✔ Buy supply wire that will connect the new panel to the meter—usually SEC cable, but if local code requires that this wire be protected with conduit, you can use individual insulated wires, which are less expensive and easier to work with. The size of the supply wire depends on the amperage of the new service *(page 124)*.

✔ Consider installing a surge arrester *(pages 60-61)* to protect your house, electrical system, and appliances from damage should lightning strike nearby power lines.

# REMOVING THE OLD BOX

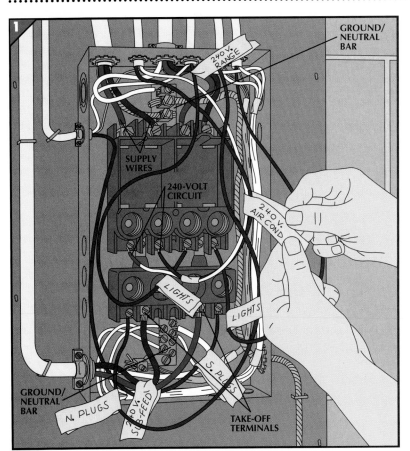

GROUND/NEUTRAL BAR

240 V. RANGE

SUPPLY WIRES

240-VOLT CIRCUIT

240 V. AIR COND

LIGHTS

LIGHTS

S. PLUGS

GROUND/NEUTRAL BAR

N. PLUGS

240 V. SUB-FEED

TAKE-OFF TERMINALS

## 1. Marking branch circuits.

◆ Shut off power at the meter *(page 65)* or at the main disconnect *(pages 62-64)*, and remove the cover of the panel.
◆ Write the function of each 120-volt circuit on a piece of tape and wrap the tape around the circuit's black, or hot, wire.
◆ For 240-volt circuits, which usually have both black and red hot wires, tape each pair together when identifying it. A white wire connected to a fuse is a hot wire for a 240-volt circuit; mark it red with paint or tape, find the black wire it is paired with by tracing the wire back to its sheathing, and tape the two together *(left)*.
◆ If a circuit serves several fixtures, mark it "Lights" to indicate general lighting.

## 2. Disconnecting the wires.

◆ Loosen the screw terminals and lugs *(right)*, and disconnect the wires.
◆ Unscrew the lock nuts fastened around cables immediately inside the box and slide the nuts off the wires; loosen the screws that secure the cables in the clamps on the outside of the box.
◆ Remove all cable staples near the box with long-nose pliers, taking care not to damage the cable sheathing.

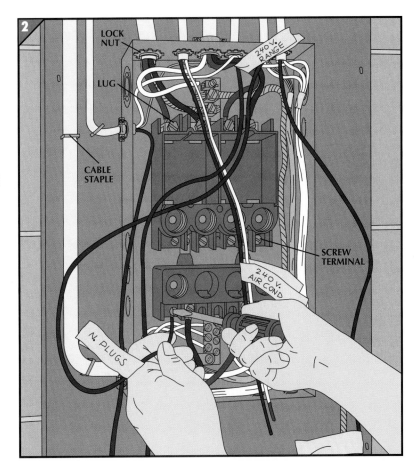

LOCK NUT

240 V. RANGE

LUG

CABLE STAPLE

SCREW TERMINAL

240 V. AIR COND

N. PLUGS

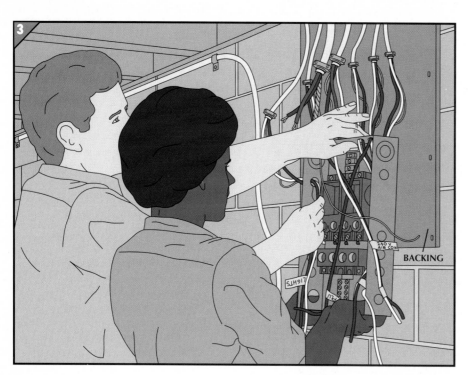

BACKING

### 3. Removing the old panel.

◆ Remove the screws that fasten the panel to the wall and, while a helper eases the panel down the wall, feed the wires out through the knockouts *(left)*.

◆ If you plan to surface-mount the new panel on the old plywood backing, make sure that it extends 8 inches beyond the new box on all sides. If it does not, replace it with a larger sheet of $\frac{3}{4}$-inch plywood.

◆ To flush-mount the new panel within a framed wall *(page 42, Step 2)*, cut a 14$\frac{1}{2}$-inch-wide hole as high as the new panel through the wall surface between two studs.

# SETTING UP THE NEW PANEL

### 1. Bonding the new panel.

If you are installing a separate main disconnect *(pages 62-64)*, you can mount the panel directly as described in Step 2 *(opposite)*. Otherwise, you must first bond the panel box to the ground/neutral block with a bonding screw or clip:

◆ If the box has a bonding screw, thread it into the predrilled hole in the box beneath the block *(right)*.

◆ If the panel has a sheet-metal bonding clip *(inset)*, screw the broad end of the clip to the box, bend the clip into a U shape with long-nose pliers, and insert the narrow end into a lug in the ground/neutral block and tighten the lug.

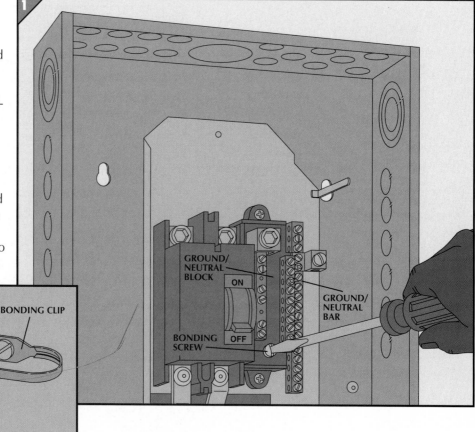

BONDING CLIP

GROUND/NEUTRAL BLOCK

ON

GROUND/NEUTRAL BAR

BONDING SCREW

OFF

## 2. Mounting the panel.

◆ To mount the panel on plywood backing, have a helper hold the box level and centered on the plywood while you mark the location of the top screw holes *(left)*.

◆ Remove the panel and drive 1½-inch round-head No. 8 wood screws partway into the wood, then slip the panel over the screws and tighten them.

◆ Make sure the box is level, then drive in the bottom screws.

To flush-mount the panel, adapt the method shown on page 42, Step 2, screwing the panel to the studs on both sides.

## 3. Grounding the panel.

◆ Check local requirements; if a second ground cable is needed—or if you are installing a separate box that houses a meter and a main disconnect *(page 50)*—consult an electrician. Ground a main-lug panel with a separate main disconnect as described on page 55.

◆ Otherwise, attach a bare stranded copper wire to the lug at the side of the ground/neutral block *(right)*. If you are using the grounding wire from the old panel, make sure its size is adequate for the new service panel.

◆ Run the wire to a grounding electrode connection *(pages 57-59)*.

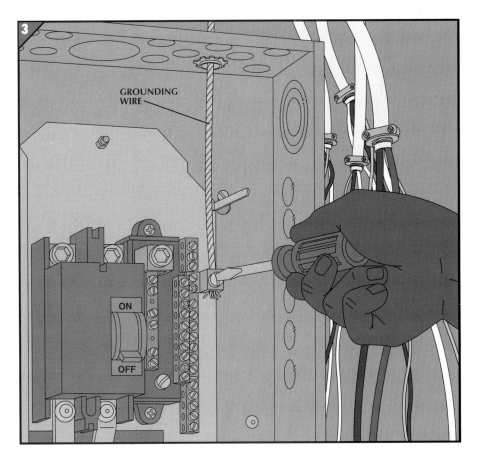

GROUNDING WIRE

# CONNECTING THE SUPPLY WIRES

### A top-feed service.

◆ If you have SEC cable entering the panel from above *(right)*, pull 18 inches through the large knockout in the top of the box, then strip the sheathing from the cable inside the box and twist the copper neutral wires together *(page 19)*.

◆ Strip 1 inch of insulation from the ends of the hot wires with an electrician's knife, work them into their lugs, then work the neutral wire into the lug on the neutral/ground block.

◆ Tighten the lugs—using a hex wrench for the panel shown; other models require a screwdriver.

◆ Secure the cable clamp at the top of the panel.

> ⚠️ *At the top of the panel, keep the neutral*
> **CAUTION** *wire well away from the hot wires and lugs to eliminate the possibility of arcing.*

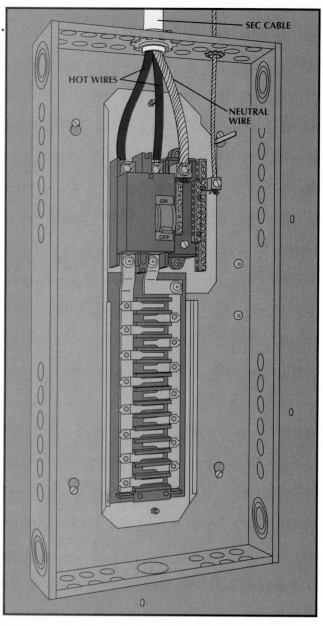

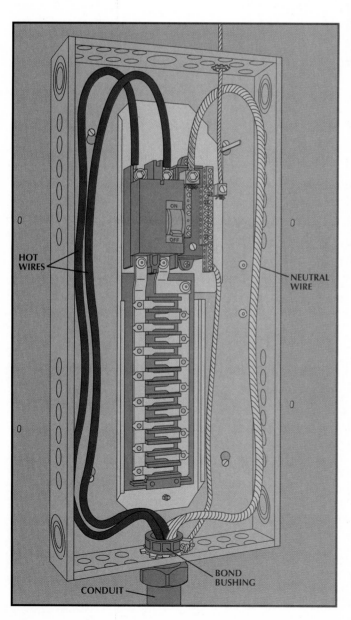

### A bottom-feed service.

◆ With supply wires that enter the panel from the bottom—most likely to be encased in steel conduit *(left)*—secure the conduit to the large knockout at the bottom of the panel with lock nuts and a bond bushing *(page 68)* and draw the wires into the box, ensuring there is enough slack to twist the copper neutral wires together *(page 19)* and reach the lugs at the top of the box.

◆ Run the hot wires up the left side of the panel to their lugs and the neutral wire up the right side to its lug.

> ⚠️ *At the top of the panel, keep the neutral*
> **CAUTION** *wire well away from the hot wires and lugs to eliminate the possibility of arcing.*

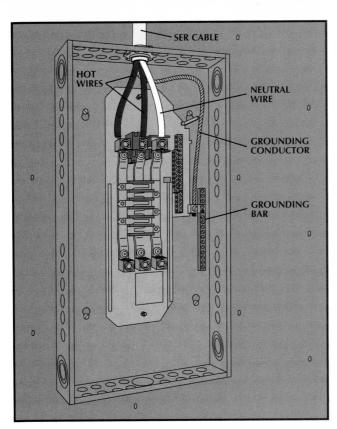

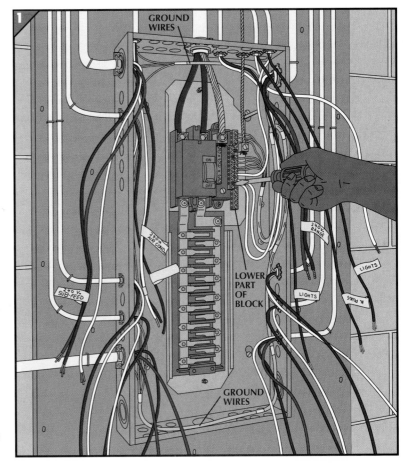

**A main-lug panel.**
For a system with a separate main disconnect *(pages 62-64)* upstream of the service panel, you can save money by buying a main-lug panel *(left)* rather than a panel with a main breaker.

◆ Install a separate grounding bar in the predrilled holes at the right side of the box.

◆ Strip the sheathing from the SER cable and the insulation from the ends of the two hot wires—either both black or black and red—and the white neutral wire *(page 19)*.

◆ Connect these wires to their lugs.

◆ Bend the fourth cable wire, a bare grounding conductor, away from the neutral lug, and run it to the upper right-hand corner of the box, then down to the large lug on the grounding bar.

# WIRING THE GROUND/NEUTRAL BLOCK AND BREAKERS

### 1. Wiring the ground/neutral block.

◆ Pull branch-circuit wires into the panel box as far as you can. If a number of the old panel's wires are too short to allow connection to the new panel, you may have to extend them with new runs of cable, connected to the old ones in junction boxes mounted next to the panel. Code prohibits splices within a panel box, although electrical inspectors usually permit one or two. If all the wires are too short, use the old panel as a junction box, connecting new lengths of cable to the old wires with wire caps and running the cables to the new panel.

◆ Install lock nuts on the cable clamps and strip any exposed cable sheathing back to the clamps.

◆ Connect each bare ground wire to a separate lug on the lower part of the ground/neutral block, bending any slack into a long loop. To bring the grounds from the far side of the panel to the block, tape them into two bundles and loop them across the top and bottom of the panel, placing them so they cannot touch hot lugs or power buses.

◆ Strip $\frac{1}{2}$ inch of insulation from each white neutral wire *(page 19)* and run them into separate lugs in the empty portion of the block *(right)*, bending the slack into loops. Tape neutrals from the far side of the panel into two bundles and run them alongside the ground wires to the block; then separate them for individual connections.

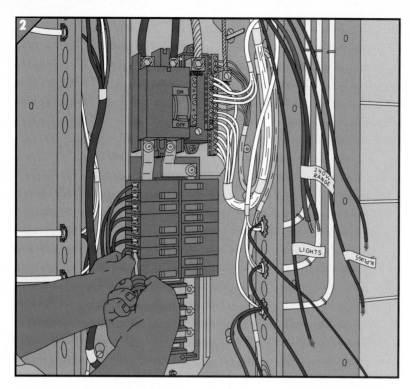

## 2. Wiring the breakers.

◆ Snap the circuit breakers into the panel and loop the hot branch-circuit wires over to their breakers, leaving as much slack as possible for later wiring changes.

◆ Strip ½ inch of insulation from the end of each hot wire *(page 19)*.

◆ Insert the wire into its breaker lug and tighten the setscrew *(left)*.

◆ Label each circuit on the chart on the panel door and remove the tape labels from the wires.

◆ Remove knockouts from the safety cover at the breaker positions.

◆ Screw the cover to the panel.

◆ With both the main and the branch-circuit breakers turned off, have the power restored at the meter. Turn the main breaker on, then the branch circuits one by one. If any of these breakers trip, switch off the main breaker, cut power to the panel, and troubleshoot the panel or circuit wiring *(pages 45-47)*.

---

### THE SPECIAL SAFEGUARD OF A GFCI

Ground-fault circuit interrupters (GFCIs) are electronic devices that react to potentially deadly leaks of electricity to ground, and disconnect the circuit in a fraction of a second. The National Electrical Code requires GFCI protection for any new outlets in electrically dangerous places—especially near water—such as bathrooms, some basement locations, kitchens within 6 feet of the sink, and out-

doors. Two versions are available. GFCI receptacles *(photograph)* are wired into outlets supplied by unprotected circuits. GFCI circuit breakers, wired into a service panel or subpanel *(right)*, protect entire circuits, combining the functions of a conventional circuit breaker and a GFCI. A GFCI breaker should be used only in a circuit limited to outlets needing ground-fault protection—the combined electrical leakages from other loads in a general-purpose circuit could cause spurious tripping. Also, if a cable run is longer than 200 feet, use a GFCI receptacle as well; natural leakage along the cable might trip a GFCI circuit breaker.

Wire a GFCI breaker as described above, connecting the black wire of the circuit to the breaker terminal marked "load power," the neutral wire to the terminal marked "load neutral," and the GFCI wire labeled "panel neutral" to a lug on the panel's neutral block. Restore the power and press the test button to simulate a ground fault. The breaker should trip immediately; reset it by flicking its switch to "On." Test the breaker at least once a month and replace it if it fails to trip.

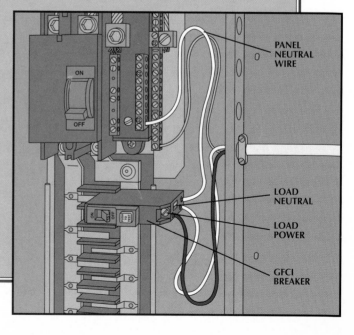

PANEL NEUTRAL WIRE

LOAD NEUTRAL

LOAD POWER

GFCI BREAKER

Your electrical system needs a ground—a bare copper cable that serves as an emergency route for surges of current produced by short circuits. The cable leads from your service panel to one or more electrodes—metal pipes or rods buried in the ground.

**Grounding Cable:** You will usually have to put in a larger cable when you upgrade your electrical service. No. 4 cable is generally the simplest to install whatever the size of your service, since most local codes require smaller cables to be specially protected or encased in conduit, but grounding requirements are highly localized and vary greatly; check local regulations before working on your system.

**Types of Electrodes:** If your old service panel was grounded to a water pipe, you can ground a new one the same way, but you must add a second ground electrode. This can be a gas pipe, if the gas company and the local code permit such a use, and if your house is supplied by underground metal pipes and a jumper wire that carries the ground path around the gas meter *(page 58, Step 2)*; otherwise the alternate ground must be a rod that is driven into the ground outside your house. The rod must be at least 8 feet long, and is generally made of $\frac{5}{8}$-inch galvanized steel. If you have plastic water pipes, or metal ones with insufficient contact with the soil, drive two grounding rods, spaced at least 6 feet apart.

If your old service panel was already grounded to a driven rod, or to a rod or copper wire extending through the concrete footing of the house foundation, you can continue to use this same ground electrode. But in such a setup, code requires that any interior metal piping be grounded as well *(page 59, bottom)*. This connection, called bonding, carries any current leaking to the pipes directly to the ground; otherwise the entire pipe system might be energized.

⚠ **CAUTION** *Grounding cable can carry current; always shut off power at the meter (page 65) or at the main disconnect (pages 62-64) before working on the grounding system.*

⚠ **CAUTION** *Before excavating a trench, locate underground obstacles such as dry wells, septic tanks, and cesspools, and electric, water, and sewer lines.*

 **TOOLS**

Screwdriver
Electric drill
Spade bit ($\frac{3}{4}$")
Shovel
Maul
Wrench
Pliers

 **MATERIALS**

Sandpaper (220-grit)
Grounding clamps
Grounding cable
Metal clamps
Grounding rod
($\frac{5}{8}$" x 8')
Acorn clamps
Pressure connectors

# CONNECTING TO UTILITY PIPES

### 1. Grounding to utility pipes.
◆ Switch off power at the meter *(page 65)* or at the main disconnect *(pages 62-64)*, then clean a 2-inch section of the cold-water pipe with 220-grit sandpaper near the point where gas and water services enter the house.
◆ Tighten a grounding clamp around the water pipe, and, if your gas company permits it, install a clamp on the metal gas pipe in the same way.
◆ Run the grounding cable from the service panel or main disconnect, securing it to the wall with a metal clamp every 3 feet, then through the nearer grounding-clamp lug and into the farther one *(inset)*, and tighten both lugs *(right)*.

If you have plastic water or gas pipes, or if the gas company does not allow grounding connections, connect to an electrode *(pages 58-59, Steps 1-2)* to provide the primary ground.

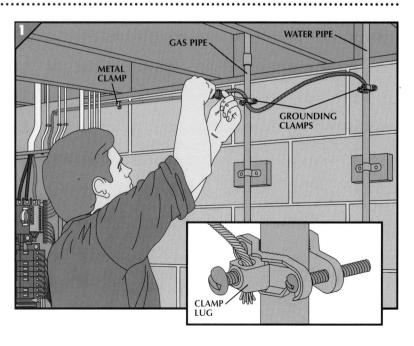

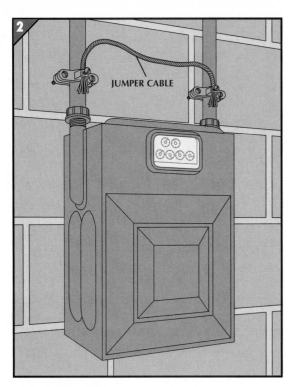

## 2. Jumping the meter.
◆ If your water or gas meter is located in the basement or outdoors within 10 feet of the house, install grounding clamps around the incoming and outgoing pipes, and run a jumping ground cable between them, leaving enough slack to allow access to the meter *(left)*. Depending on the meter's location, you can jump it with the grounding cable from the panel.
◆ Install jumpers in the same way to span any plastic-pipe splices in a run of metal pipe.
◆ Label the cable with a red cardboard tag so no one will be tempted to disconnect it.

No jumpers are needed for meters and plastic-pipe splices farther than 10 feet from the house.

# GROUNDING TO A BURIED ROD OUTSIDE

## 1. Driving the grounding rod.
◆ Working inside, drill a $\frac{3}{4}$-inch hole through the wall as close to the service panel as possible and through the band joist and siding just above the foundation. Locate the hole farther from the panel, if necessary, to avoid hitting underground obstacles when burying the grounding rod. If the rod you plan to drive will serve as the primary ground and you have an exterior main disconnect, locate the hole near the disconnect box.
◆ Feed the grounding cable through the hole.
◆ Outside, dig a 1-foot-deep trench into the ground directly in front of the cable, stopping 18 inches from the foundation.
◆ Holding the grounding rod at the end of the trench, drive it straight down with a maul *(right)* until the top end is below ground level. If the rod hits a rock, pull it up and drive it in at a 45-degree angle, or clamp the cable to the rod *(Step 2)* and bury the assembly horizontally in a trench at least $2\frac{1}{2}$ feet deep.
◆ If you need a second grounding rod—such as when the first rod is the primary ground—continue the trench at least 6 feet out from the house and drive another rod 6 feet from the first one in the same way.

58

## 2. Connecting the wire to the rod.

◆ Slide an acorn clamp approved for direct burial *(photograph)* onto the grounding rod.

◆ Run the grounding cable down the foundation wall and along the bottom of the trench to the rod. Fit the cable between the rod and the end of the clamp opposite the bolt, then tighten the bolt against the rod with a wrench *(right)*. If there is a second grounding rod, run the same cable to it and attach it in the same way with an acorn clamp.

◆ Cut off excess cable at the rod with pliers and backfill the trench.

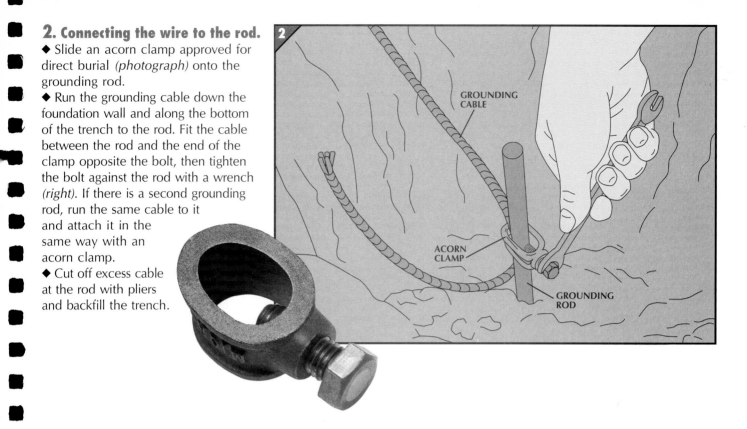

GROUNDING CABLE

ACORN CLAMP

GROUNDING ROD

# HOOKING UP TO A BUILT-IN ELECTRODE

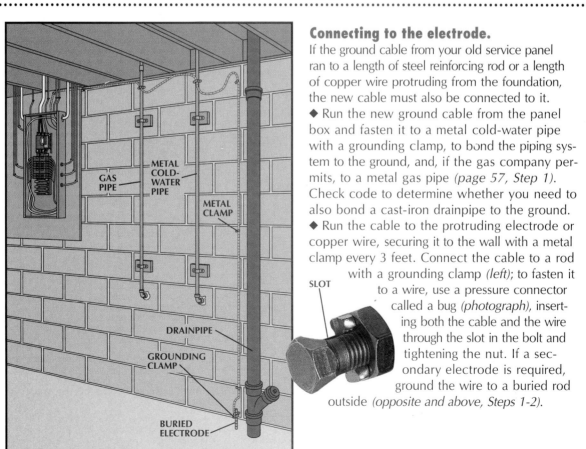

GAS PIPE

METAL COLD-WATER PIPE

METAL CLAMP

DRAINPIPE

GROUNDING CLAMP

BURIED ELECTRODE

SLOT

### Connecting to the electrode.

If the ground cable from your old service panel ran to a length of steel reinforcing rod or a length of copper wire protruding from the foundation, the new cable must also be connected to it.

◆ Run the new ground cable from the panel box and fasten it to a metal cold-water pipe with a grounding clamp, to bond the piping system to the ground, and, if the gas company permits, to a metal gas pipe *(page 57, Step 1)*. Check code to determine whether you need to also bond a cast-iron drainpipe to the ground.

◆ Run the cable to the protruding electrode or copper wire, securing it to the wall with a metal clamp every 3 feet. Connect the cable to a rod with a grounding clamp *(left)*; to fasten it to a wire, use a pressure connector called a bug *(photograph)*, inserting both the cable and the wire through the slot in the bolt and tightening the nut. If a secondary electrode is required, ground the wire to a buried rod outside *(opposite and above, Steps 1-2)*.

# Blocking a Bolt of Lightning

When lightning hits a power line, a pulse of enormous voltage courses along the line in a few millionths of a second. Devices called lightning-surge arresters on the power lines usually block voltage spikes, but if an arrester fails or if lightning strikes between your home and the nearest arrester, your television set may explode, electricity may arc out of receptacles, and switch and breaker contacts may fuse. Even underground services are vulnerable—lightning that strikes a tree often jumps from the roots to underground cables.

**Protection at the Service Panel:** You can protect your house from surges by wiring a lightning-surge arrester to your service panel *(below)*. The arrester shunts surges safely to ground before they can enter your electrical system. It does not, however, protect your house from direct lightning strikes—only a professionally installed lightning-rod system can do that.

An arrester works like a pressure-relief valve in a steam system. It has a connection to ground, an escape route that includes a space called a spark gap. The resistance of the gap is sufficient to keep ordinary currents from escaping to ground; such currents flow past the arrester without hindrance. But a very high voltage, such as that produced by lightning, jumps the gap, permitting the surge current to drain away to ground.

While a lightning-surge arrester safeguards house wiring against spikes of 2,000 volts or more, lesser voltages can harm electronic equipment such as television sets and personal computers. Protect these appliances from smaller surges with an isolated-ground receptacle or a plug-in surge protector *(opposite)*.

⚠️ **CAUTION** *Always shut off power at the meter (page 65) or at the main disconnect (pages 62-64) before working on the service panel.*

**TOOLS**

Hammer
Nail set
Pliers
Screwdriver
Multipurpose
   tool

# INSTALLING A SURGE ARRESTER

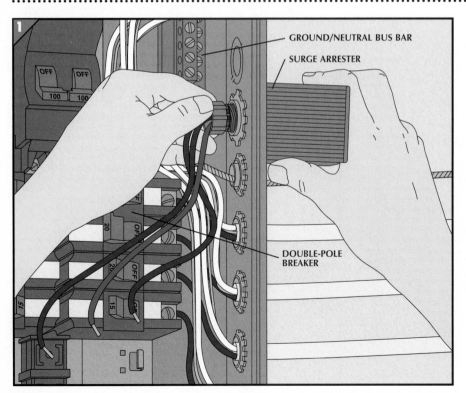

GROUND/NEUTRAL BUS BAR

SURGE ARRESTER

DOUBLE-POLE BREAKER

**1. Mounting the arrester.**
◆ Turn off power to the panel at the meter *(page 65)* or at the main disconnect *(pages 62-64)*, unscrew the panel cover, and remove a knockout on the side of the box *(pages 37-38)* close to both the ground/neutral bus bar and a double-pole breaker. The breaker need not be unused; the arrester can share its terminals with the wires of any 240-volt circuit.
◆ Insert the surge arrester's wires and threaded fitting in the knockout hole and fasten it to the box with its lock nut *(left)*.

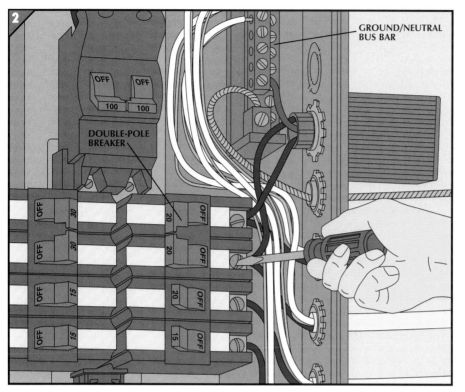

GROUND/NEUTRAL BUS BAR

OFF OFF
100 100

DOUBLE-POLE BREAKER

OFF 30
OFF 30
OFF 15
OFF 15

20
20
20
15

OFF
OFF
OFF
OFF

## 2. Wiring the arrester.

◆ Cut the surge arrester's green ground wire to a length that will allow it to run to a terminal on the ground/neutral bus bar without excessive slack. Strip the insulation from the end of the wire *(page 19)* and fasten it to the terminal.

◆ Connect the arrester's two black leads to the load side of the double-pole breaker in the same way *(left)*.

◆ Replace the panel cover and restore the power.

## PROTECTING EQUIPMENT FROM VOLTAGE SPIKES

To protect electronic equipment such as personal computers, televisions, and microwave ovens from power surges, you can install an isolated-ground circuit and receptacle *(right)*. A 120-volt, 15-amp circuit, an isolated-ground circuit uses three-conductor cable and a special orange-colored receptacle that has an insulated grounding screw. The black wire runs from the receptacle's load terminal directly to the circuit breaker in the service panel without going through any other receptacles or switches. The neutral white wire runs from the receptacle's line terminal to the ground/neutral bar in the panel. The ground wire is attached to the bonding screw in the receptacle's outlet box and to the ground/neutral bar in the service panel. The red wire, tagged with green tape because it serves as an additional grounding wire, runs from the receptacle's grounding screw to the ground/neutral bar.

For a less permanent solution, you can plug an electronic apparatus into a surge protector. Available at computer stores, the protector can then be plugged into any grounded outlet, safeguarding the equipment from the voltage spikes.

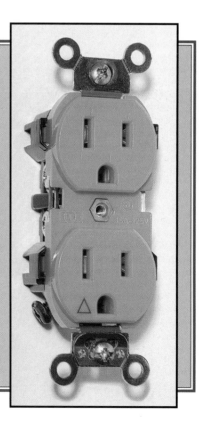

# A Shutdown for Safety

**A** main shutdown or disconnect, with fuses or circuit breakers that can stop the flow of current throughout a house, is an important safeguard. The National Electrical Code requires that these disconnecting devices be installed near the point where power enters your house. You do have a choice, though, on its precise placement.

**Positioning the Disconnect:** Most main disconnects are placed inside the service panel, above the smaller fuses or breakers that protect individual branch circuits. This arrangement has disadvantages. If the service panel is installed in a basement, it will be difficult to access in the darkness should fuses blow or breakers trip. Also, even when the main breakers or fuses are shut down, the terminals of the main disconnect in the panel are still hot; to work on the panel, you will have to shut off power at the meter *(page 65)*.

In a more convenient arrangement, the main disconnect is set in a small separate panel of its own near the meter, and a cable links the disconnect to a subpanel containing the breakers or fuses of the branch circuits. You can cut all power at the disconnect and work safely on branch circuits in the subpanel. The subpanel can be placed wherever you choose, for the connecting cable from the main disconnect can run to any room. And if you have the meter moved, it will be easier to install a main disconnect box at the new location than to move the entire service panel.

If you are installing a disconnect and a new meter at the same time, have the service disconnected and the new meter installed, then hook up the disconnect *(pages 66-67)* before the service is restored.

> ⚠️ **CAUTION** *Have the electric company turn the power off at the pole before mounting a main disconnect.*

---

 **TOOLS**
Screwdriver
Electric drill
Hacksaw · Hole saw
Hammer · Electrician's
Nail set · knife
Pliers · Hex wrench

**MATERIALS**
Main disconnect box
PVC conduit (2")
and fittings
PVC solvent cement
Wood screws (1½" No. 12)
Cable clamp and lock nut
SEC and SER cable
Grounding bus bar
Sealing compound

 **SAFETY TIPS**
*Goggles protect your eyes when you are drilling.*

---

## A MAIN-DISCONNECT PANEL

Small main-disconnect panels are available at electrical-supply stores as conventional boxes for indoors *(right)* or as weatherproof boxes for the outside installation shown opposite. With boxes intended for outdoor use, be sure that the model you buy can be padlocked through flanges on the bottom so no one can turn off the power—or turn it on while you are working at the subpanel.

The main disconnect is usually connected to the meter box by polyvinyl chloride (PVC) conduit *(page 68)* containing two insulated hot wires and a bare neutral wire—the same three wires that run through an SEC cable. Since these wires are enclosed by the conduit, you can safely strip the cable sheathing from them and push them through the conduit individually. Power flows from the main disconnect to the branch-circuit panel through SER cable—two hot wires, an insulated white neutral wire, and a bare wire that grounds the service panel to that of the main disconnect. Check local codes; you may be required to run the SER cable through conduit. As the primary power panel, the disconnect must be grounded with the rest of your electrical system *(page 64, Step 4)*.

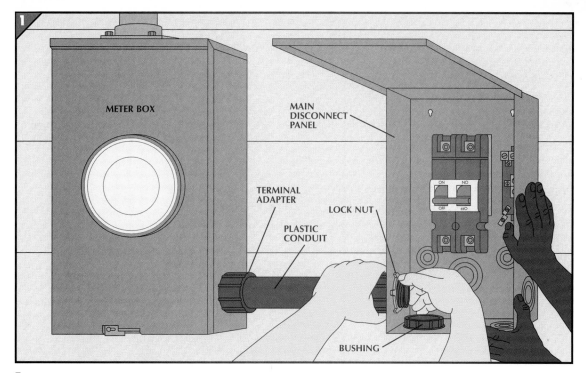

## 1. Installing the box.

◆ With a hacksaw, cut a 12-inch length of 2-inch PVC conduit, then glue a threaded terminal adapter to each end *(page 68)*.

◆ Remove a side knockout from a main-disconnect panel and the meter box *(pages 37-38)* and with a helper holding the disconnect panel, join the conduit assembly to the boxes with a lock nut and bushing *(above)*.

◆ Fasten the disconnect panel to the wall, driving 1½-inch No. 12 wood screws into studs for a wall with siding; drill holes for anchors to screw into a masonry wall.

◆ Remove the sheathing from an SEC cable *(page 19)* that is the correct size for the service-panel amperage *(page 124)* and run the separate wires through the conduit; allow for 16 inches of wire in each box.

◆ Do not connect the wires in the meter box.

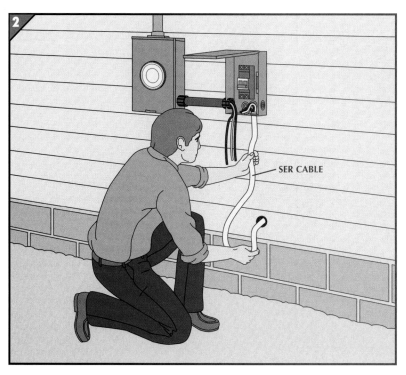

## 2. Running the cable.

◆ Drill a 2¼-inch hole through the house wall *(pages 71-72)* in line with the band joist.

◆ Cut a length of 2-inch PVC plastic conduit as long as the wall is thick, then insert the conduit into the hole so the ends are flush with the wall surfaces.

◆ Remove a knockout from the bottom of the main disconnect box and connect a length of SER cable—leaving at least 16 inches of cable in the box—with a lock nut inside the box and a cable clamp outside.

◆ Feed the SER cable through the wall to the service panel inside *(left)*.

◆ Strip 14 inches of sheathing from the cable *(page 19)*, exposing the insulated white neutral wire, the two hot wires, and the bare wire.

## 3. Wiring the disconnect.

◆ Cut the SEC and SER wires to reach their setscrew connectors without excessive slack.

◆ Strip 1 inch of insulation from the black and white wires, and twist the bare wires into continuous strands *(page 19)*.

◆ Fasten the bare SEC neutral wire to the connector at the right of the disconnect panel, using a hex wrench to tighten the screw that holds the wire *(right)*.

◆ Attach the white SER neutral wire to the connector below the bare neutral wire in the same way.

◆ Fasten the black SEC hot wires to the connectors at the top center of the panel and attach the black SER hot wires to the connectors at the bottom.

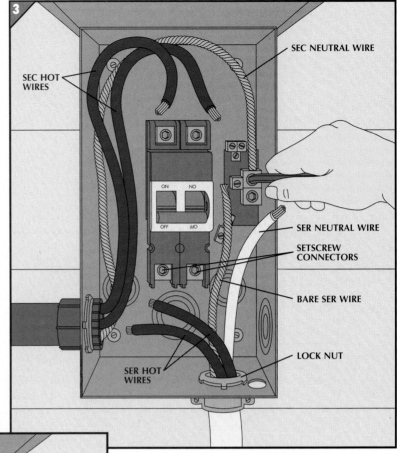

SEC HOT WIRES

SEC NEUTRAL WIRE

SER NEUTRAL WIRE

SETSCREW CONNECTORS

BARE SER WIRE

LOCK NUT

SER HOT WIRES

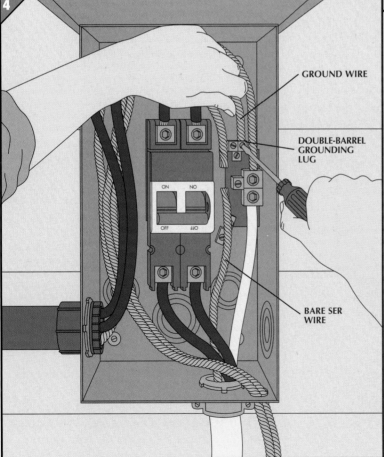

GROUND WIRE

DOUBLE-BARREL GROUNDING LUG

BARE SER WIRE

## 4. Grounding the system.

◆ Run the wires from the electrical-system grounding electrodes *(pages 57-59)* through the hole in the house wall alongside the SER cable and into the disconnect box through the hole for the ground wire at the bottom of the box. (If the box lacks such a hole, drill one.)

◆ Loop the wires around the left side of the box and under the black SEC wires, and attach them to the double-barrel grounding lug *(left)*. Check the code for local grounding requirements.

◆ Disconnect the ground wires from the service panel and remove the bonding screw from the panel *(page 52, Step 1)*.

◆ Install a new grounding bar *(page 55, top)* in the service panel and run the ground wires to it.

◆ Attach the bare SER wire to the connector directly below the one you used for the ground wires in the main disconnect; attach the other end of this wire to the new grounding bar in the service panel.

◆ Outside the box, tie the ground wires to the SER cable with plastic tie wraps. Seal the gaps between the cable and the conduit, and between the conduit and the house wall, with sealing compound. Have an electrician or the electric company wire the meter before restoring the power.

To measure the power coming into a house, the electric company installs a meter in the line between the power cables and the service panel. When you need to interrupt the current to a service panel or main disconnect, a licensed electrician will have to disengage the meter.

The meter is mounted in a chassis that resembles a large plug; the prongs of the plug fit into a meter socket permanently mounted on a house wall. When electricians remove this plug they say they are "pulling the meter."

Before pulling a meter, an electrician first turns off the main circuit breakers or pulls the main fuses in the service panel. Then, standing on a sheet of $\frac{3}{4}$-inch plywood covered with a rubber mat to insulate him from the ground, and wearing thick rubber gloves certified by the Underwriters Laboratories (UL), he cuts a twisted wire seal that locks a collar clamp around the meter. Next, he removes the clamp screw with a plastic-handled screwdriver, opens the collar, and pulls it away from the meter *(right, top)*.

To remove the meter, the electrician grasps it on both sides and pulls it down and out to release it from the clips in the socket *(right, middle)*. As soon as the meter is free, he immediately inserts a glass safety plate into the old meter collar, sets the assembly over the exposed meter socket *(right, bottom)*, and screws the collar clamp back into place. The glass plate is essential to keep anyone from touching the hot terminals in the socket.

Finally, he checks the service panel with a voltage tester to be sure that the power has been cut off inside the house. If it has not, the electric company must check the panel and meter before any further work is done.

⚠️ **CAUTION** *Do not attempt the job yourself— the power that flows through the meter is unfused and extremely dangerous. Contact the electric company to determine who is authorizerd to pull the meter in your area: either the company itself or a licensed electrician.*

METER BOX

65

When a service panel is upgraded from 60 amps to 100, 200, or more *(pages 50-56)*, the power company must also change the meter to handle the increased power load.

**Managing the Project:** The jobs of upgrading the meter and panel should be done at the same time. If local codes and your utility company allow it, you can save money by mounting the meter socket yourself. When the socket is ready and the new panel is installed, have an electrician hook up temporary service by detouring power through the old meter into the new meter socket. After its final inspection, the power company will take out the old meter and hook up the new one.

**Obtaining Materials:** Get a meter socket and box designed to handle the increased amperage, as well as weatherproof connectors for the service cable from the utility company. Buy the new cable and cable clamps to pin the cable to the wall of your house at an electrical-supply store. You'll need certain specialized tools if you have a masonry wall: a twist drill or an electric hammer drill, and a drive-pin set.

 **CAUTION** *While temporary service is in operation, do not use more amperage than your old service panel could handle—doing so may overload the old supply lines from the utility company's transformer.*

 **TOOLS**

Solenoid voltage tester

Level
Hammer
Twist drill
Drive-pin set

**MATERIALS**

Meter socket and box
Screw anchors
Wood screws ($1\frac{1}{2}$" or 2" No. 12)
Sealing compound

SEC cable
Weatherproof connector
Lock nut
Metal clamps
Drive pins (1")
Round-head wood screws (1" No. 8)

**SAFETY TIPS**

*Goggles protect your eyes when you are drilling or hammering into masonry or wood.*

## MOUNTING A METER SOCKET

### 1. Mounting the new socket.

◆ Have an electrician pull the meter *(page 65)*.
◆ Test the hot and neutral leads in the service panel to make sure that all power to the house is off *(page 36)*, then disconnect the service cable from the panel and pull it out through the wall.
◆ Set the new meter box against the wall, 12 to 18 inches away from the old meter and 3 to 6 feet above the ground. Level and plumb the box, mark its screw holes on the wall, then remove it.
◆ For a masonry wall, set the tip of a twist drill against one of the marks and hammer the handle until the bit is engaged *(right)*. Twist the drill 60 degrees clockwise and strike again. Twist and strike until you have a hole 2 inches deep, then repeat the procedure at the other marks.
◆ Position the box over the holes and fasten it to the wall with screw anchors and $1\frac{1}{2}$-inch No. 12 wood screws.

In a wooden wall, fasten the meter box with 2-inch No. 12 wood screws.

OLD METER BOX

OLD SEC CABLE

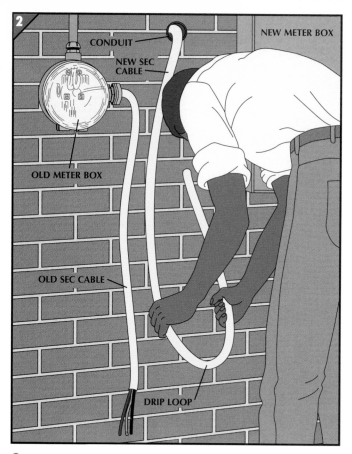

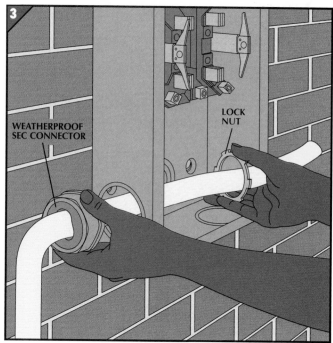

## 2. Making a service drip.

Insert a length of conduit into the hole in the house wall left by the old cable *(page 63, Step 2)*, then pull about 8 feet of SEC cable from the new service panel out of the house through the conduit. Bend the cable down toward the ground, then up to the new meter box in a curve that lies flat against the wall to create a "drip loop" that prevents rainwater from flowing into the box *(above)*.

## 3. Connecting the cable.

◆ Slide a weatherproof SEC connector 18 inches up the free end of the new SEC cable. Tighten the connector firmly around the cable, then push the cable through the hole in the side of the new meter box until the connector contacts the box.

◆ Slide a lock nut over the end of the cable *(above)* and tighten it around the threads of the weatherproof connector.

◆ Push about 18 inches of the old service entrance cable through the hole in the top of the box and pack the hole with sealing compound.

## 4. Securing the cables.

◆ Set a metal clamp over the drip loop in the new SEC cable, position a 1-inch pin over the hole in the clamp, and strike the head of the drive-pin set sharply with a hammer to drive the pin into a mortar joint of a brick or concrete-block wall *(left)*. On a wooden wall, fasten the clamps with 1-inch round-head No. 8 wood screws.

◆ Install as many clamps as necessary to hold the cable firmly against the wall.

◆ Seal the gap between the cable and the conduit with sealing compound, and between the conduit and the house wall with patching concrete.

# Protecting Conductors with Conduit

Whenever you run cable outdoors in locations where it could be damaged, you need to protect it with a covering known as conduit. Map out the route that the conduit will follow to find out what type is best for the job, and what fittings and connectors *(below)* you will need. In general, use 2-inch conduit; 1-inch for a circuit of less than 100 amps.

**Three Types:** Conduit of galvanized steel, called rigid or heavy-wall conduit, is strong and corrosion resistant, making it particularly suitable for runs subject to mechanical abuse, the weight of vehicles, or bad weather. It comes in 10-foot lengths threaded at each end; sections are joined together with threaded couplings.

Thin-wall steel conduit called electrical mechanical tubing (EMT), light and easy to work with, is suited for relatively protected locations such as a run from a meter to an outside panel. It is sold in unthreaded 10-foot lengths and is linked by couplings with setscrews that tighten to hold the fittings in place.

The least expensive and the easiest to work with, polyvinyl chloride (PVC) is best used aboveground; if it will be exposed to direct sunlight, cover it with two coats of latex paint to prevent deterioration. PVC comes in unthreaded, 10-foot lengths that are joined with glued fittings. To connect pieces, first coat the matching surfaces with PVC primer, then with PVC cement. Insert the conduit into the fitting and give the pieces a quarter-turn to ensure a secure bond.

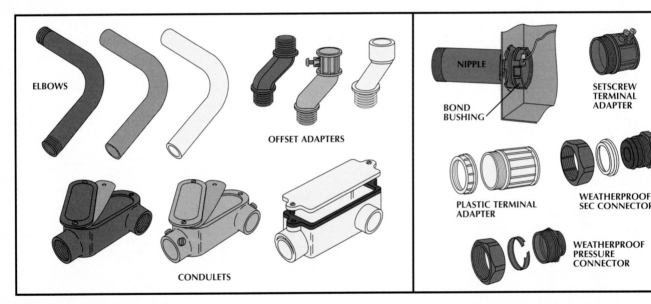

ELBOWS

OFFSET ADAPTERS

CONDULETS

NIPPLE

BOND BUSHING

SETSCREW TERMINAL ADAPTER

PLASTIC TERMINAL ADAPTER

WEATHERPROOF SEC CONNECTOR

WEATHERPROOF PRESSURE CONNECTOR

## Fittings and connectors.

The three types of conduit have corresponding fittings and connectors; in the illustration above, they are shown as dark blue (steel), gray (EMT), and tan (PVC).

Some fittings enable you to route cable around bends *(above, left)*. For 90- or 45-degree angles above or below ground, use an elbow. A condulet, which can be opened, bends cable easily around a turn, but is limited to above-ground use. Where you need to route wire around an obstacle, use an offset adapter.

In addition to the standard couplings that join straight runs of conduit, other connectors are employed to secure conduit at knockouts in boxes *(above, right)*. At a service panel or meter box, secure a steel nipple—4 to 36 inches long and threaded at both ends—an elbow, or other threaded fitting by lock nuts screwed against the inside and outside of the box; ground it

with a bond bushing—a metal bushing fitted with a copper lug. (In service panels and main disconnects, connect the lug to the neutral bus bar with a ground wire. Inside meter boxes, run the ground wire to a second lug screwed to the metal box.) A threaded setscrew terminal adapter links EMT conduit or a cut end of rigid conduit to panel boxes or condulets, held in place with lock nuts and a bond bushing if necessary; its PVC counterpart is a plastic terminal adapter, which does not need grounding and has its own lock nut.

A weatherproof pressure connector joins unthreaded conduit in damp locations; tightening the nut squeezes a metal flange around the conduit to form a waterproof seal. Run unprotected SEC cable in and out of boxes with weatherproof SEC connectors, in which a rubber ring is squeezed around the cable when the connector is tightened; add a lock nut to complete the connection.

| | | |
|---|---|---|
| Vise | Electric drill | Cold chisel |
| Hacksaw | Masonry bit | Maul |
| Pipe cutter | Extension bit | Punch |
| Half-round file | Hole saw | |
| Utility knife | Hammer drill | |

Conduit and fittings
Solvent cement
Patching concrete
Sealing compound

*Wear goggles when drilling or chiseling through concrete blocks.*

# THREE BASIC ROUTES

### Down from above.
In a wall-mounted service *(pages 74-76)*, cable runs into the top of the meter through a weatherproof SEC connector. A second cable runs out of the meter and into a condulet, protected in this example by EMT conduit. The unthreaded EMT is connected to the condulet and meter with setscrew terminal adapters secured with lock nuts and a bond bushing. The cable runs through the house wall to the service panel in a rigid conduit nipple, which screws into the condulet and panel box. Lock nuts and a bond bushing secure the conduit to the service panel. The hole in the wall is sealed with patching concrete and the end of the nipple waterproofed with sealing compound.

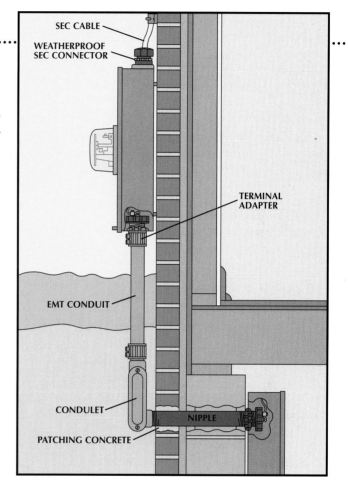

SEC CABLE
WEATHERPROOF SEC CONNECTOR
TERMINAL ADAPTER
EMT CONDUIT
CONDULET
NIPPLE
PATCHING CONCRETE

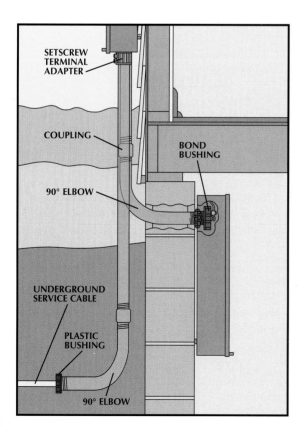

SETSCREW TERMINAL ADAPTER
COUPLING
BOND BUSHING
90° ELBOW
UNDERGROUND SERVICE CABLE
PLASTIC BUSHING
90° ELBOW

### Up from below.
An underground service-entrance cable, which must be protected by steel conduit, turns upward in a 90-degree galvanized-steel elbow, connected in this example to a 4-foot length of rigid conduit that runs up the house wall into the meter box. At the lower end of the elbow, sealing compound waterproofs the conduit and a threaded plastic bushing protects the cable from abrasion. The vertical conduit, cut from a 10-foot length, has no threads on the upper end; a setscrew terminal adapter connects it to the meter box. Inside the box, it is grounded with a bond bushing. In a similar conduit-elbow arrangement, a second cable leaves the meter through conduit, enters the house above grade, and runs into the service panel through a 90-degree elbow secured to the box with two lock nuts and a bond bushing.

## A single nipple.

In this mast-style service entrance *(pages 77-78)*, cable runs into the top of the meter through metal conduit. When a service panel is mounted inside the house directly opposite the meter outside, the two boxes can be joined by cable running through the house wall in a rigid-conduit nipple. The nipple is connected to each box with two lock nuts and a bond bushing. The gaps around the nipple are sealed with patching concrete.

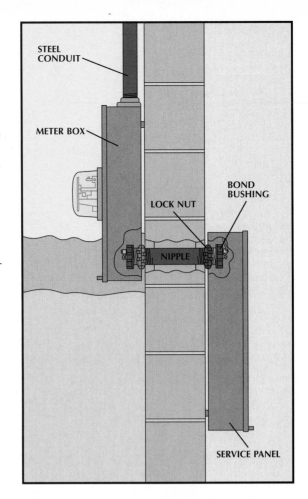

# CUTTING CONDUIT TO FIT

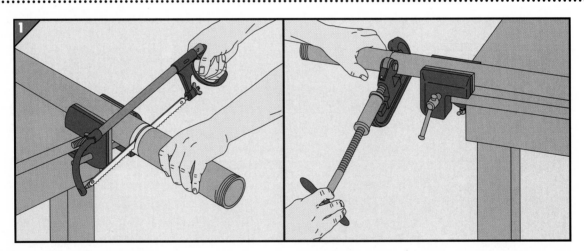

## 1. Sawing and cutting conduit.

You can cut conduit with a hacksaw, but if you have many lengths to fit, you can save time with a pipe cutter *(page 9)*.
◆ Secure the conduit in a vise.
◆ Fit a hacksaw with an 18-teeth-per-inch blade for rigid conduit, or 32 teeth per inch for EMT and plastic conduit.
◆ Wrap a length of masking tape around the conduit to prevent the saw from slipping—overlap the ends of the tape—and mark the tape at the cutting point.
◆ Begin sawing with the hacksaw blade parallel to the floor; then, after a few strokes, angle the blade toward the floor. If the blade sticks, press down on the projecting end of

the conduit with your free hand to open the cut a little *(above, left)*.

With a metal-conduit pipe cutter, tighten the jaws of the tool around the conduit until the cutting wheel presses on it *(above, right)*. Swing the cutter completely around the conduit and tighten the jaws again to dig the wheel more deeply into the metal. Repeat until the conduit breaks in two.

For PVC, fit the jaws of a plastic-pipe cutter around the conduit and squeeze the handles together until the jaws sever the conduit.

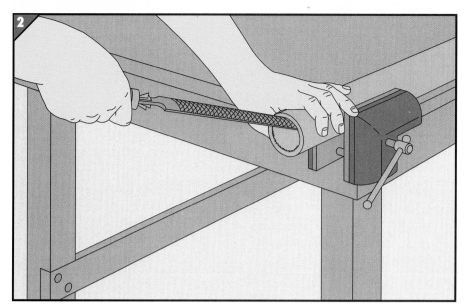

### 2. Removing the burrs.

Smooth the burrs on the cut end of rigid conduit or EMT with a half-round file *(left)*.

On plastic conduit, cut the burrs off with a sharp utility knife, then bevel the outside edges of the conduit to fit into a coupling for gluing with solvent cement.

# A PASSAGEWAY THROUGH A HOUSE WALL

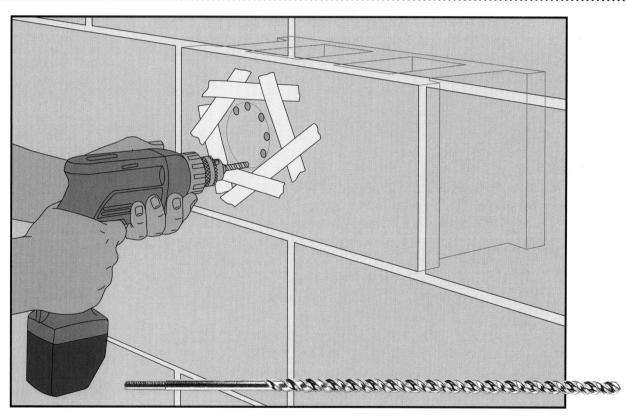

### In concrete block.

◆ Outline the end of a piece of conduit on a block midway between horizontal mortar joints about a third of the way across the block—which is where a hollow core is likely to be.
◆ Apply masking tape around the outline to minimize cracking, then drill a series of holes with a $\frac{1}{4}$-inch masonry bit just inside the outline *(above)*.
◆ Break out the spaces between the holes with a cold chisel and maul, creating a large hole.

◆ Center an extension bit *(photograph)* in the large hole and drill through the inside of the house wall.
◆ On the interior wall, use the extension-bit hole as a centerpoint to scribe a circle the size of the conduit with a compass.
◆ Complete the conduit hole as you did the exterior one.
◆ Push the conduit through the wall and seal it in place with patching concrete.

### Through wood.

◆ Locate the studs, then, with a hole saw, drill a hole as wide as the conduit in the exterior wall between two studs *(right)*.

◆ Remove any insulation in the path of the conduit hole, then center an extension bit in the hole, drill a pilot hole through the interior wall, and complete the conduit hole inside the house.

◆ Push a nipple through the wall so the threads protrude on both sides and tighten lock nuts on the ends.

◆ Waterproof the inside and outside of the wall with sealing compound.

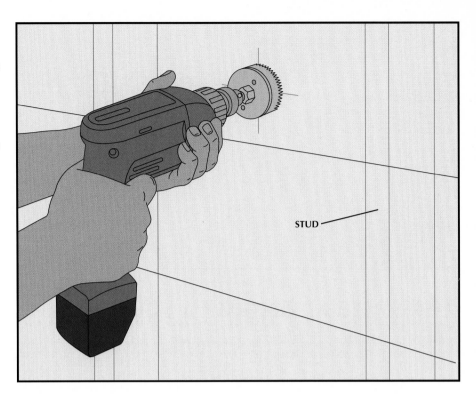

STUD

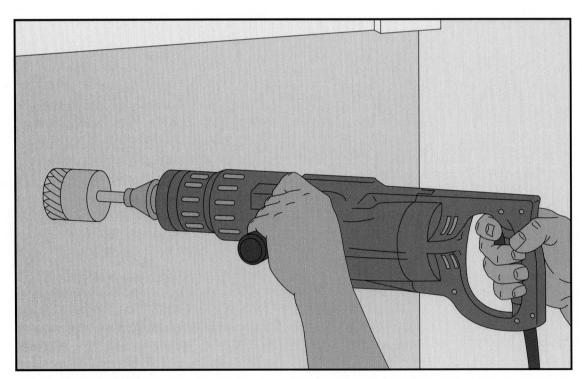

### In concrete.

◆ Start the hole with a punch.

◆ Deepen the hole with a heavy-duty hammer drill fitted with a carbide-tipped hole saw as wide as the conduit *(above)*. Apply heavy pressure until the hole saw jams in the concrete, then retract the hole saw from the wall and chisel out the concrete at the center of the hole. Repeat the technique with the drill and chisel as necessary to cut completely through the wall.

To bring power to a meter, the electric company runs a group of wires called a service drop from its overhead supply lines to a point where a splice can be made to the SEC cable.

**The Service Drop:** Older three-wire service drops consist of three separate wires; newer ones, called triplex, have a bare neutral wire with two insulated hot wires wrapped around it.

The connections are made through a two-part overhead service: a set of insulators that support the service drop, and a metal hood, called a weatherhead, that protects the cable from moisture. If you move your meter, you may have to move both the insulators and the weatherhead. If you upgrade your service panel *(pages 50-56)*, you will have to replace the meter, SEC cable, and weatherhead with equipment that can handle the increased amperage.

The electric company may do part of this work: In many areas it will attend to the overhead equipment when you install a new meter socket. If it will not, ask one of its representatives about the location of the new service: Electrical codes set restrictions on the distance a cable can run from a utility pole to a house. Where your new service location is too far from the pole, you may have to run the cable underground *(pages 79-81)*. If you have three-wire service, you may want the company to replace it with triplex. When you are replacing your meter, have the company disconnect the service at the pole.

**Locating the Weatherhead:** At the house, the position of the new weatherhead and insulators must conform to code: usually at least 3 feet away from windows, porches, and fire escapes, and any wires running across your property need to be at least 10 feet above lawns and patios, 12 feet above driveways, and 18 feet above streets and alleys. If you raise a mast above the roof *(pages 77-78)* to reach the height required by code, the supply wires have to run at least 18 inches above the roof and no more than 4 feet across it.

⚠️ **CAUTION** *Never work near a live service drop while you set up an overhead service—have the electric company cut off power.*

**TOOLS**

| | |
|---|---|
| Chalk line | Electric drill |
| Ruler | Drive-pin set |
| Screwdriver | Electrician's knife |
| | Plumb bob |
| | Pry bar |

**MATERIALS**

| | |
|---|---|
| Common nails (3½") | Weatherproof connector |
| Wood screws (1½" No. 8) | Roofing cement |
| Lag screws (⅜" x 6") | Roofing nails (1½") |
| SEC cable | Galvanized-steel conduit |
| Circular clamps | Offset circular clamps |
| Weatherhead and support bracket | Ceramic insulator |
| Insulator rack | Guy wire and turnbuckle |
| Roof jack | |
| Insulator clamp | |

**SAFETY TIPS**

*Protect your eyes with goggles when using a drill.*

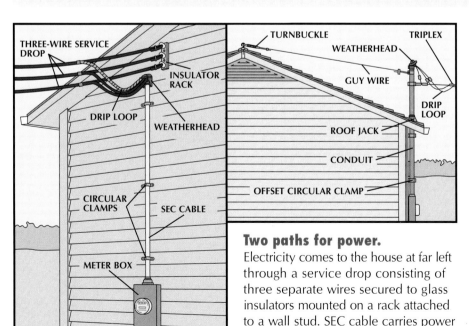

## Two paths for power.

Electricity comes to the house at far left through a service drop consisting of three separate wires secured to glass insulators mounted on a rack attached to a wall stud. SEC cable carries power through conduit down the wall to the meter. Connections between the drop and the cable are made with wire clamps called bugs. The cable wires run to a waterproof metal weatherhead through a drip loop. The sheathed cable between the weatherhead and the meter is secured by circular clamps.

In the house at near left, the drop (in this case, a triplex) and the weatherhead are mounted on a service mast, a 2-inch steel conduit extending through the roof. A guy wire and turnbuckle help support the mast; a collar called a roof jack prevents water from running down the conduit to the meter. Below the roof, offset circular clamps hold the conduit 1 inch away from the house to align it with the entrance hole on the top of the meter box.

**WEATHERHEAD**

**OFFSET CIRCULAR METAL CLAMP**

**ROOF JACK**

**CERAMIC INSULATOR**

Many electrical-supply stores carry complete kits for setting up an overhead service. The items at left are included in a typical kit for a mast-style service *(pages 77-78)*. If you must buy the parts separately, get enough SEC cable to run from the meter to the weatherhead, plus an additional 5 feet for connections; clamps to secure the cable to the wall; a new weatherhead; and one or more glass or ceramic insulators. For the mast, buy steel conduit (normally 2 inches in diameter for a 150-amp service or more, or for any drop longer than 60 feet; $1\frac{1}{4}$ inches for 100 amps or less), offset circular metal clamps to hold the conduit to the house wall, a galvanized-metal roof jack to weatherproof the hole for the mast, and a steel guy wire to support a mast more than 3 feet high. For a wall-mounted triplex service *(below and pages 75-76)*, the roof jack is omitted, but you will need a special eyebolt, provided by the electric company, to anchor the service wires to the wall.

# A WALL-MOUNTED LINE

## 1. Aligning the cable.

◆ Drop a chalk line to serve as a plumb bob from the new weatherhead location to the center of the knockout in the top of the meter box. Have a helper set a ruler across the knockout to center the point of the chalk line case *(right)*, then snap the chalk line from the weatherhead position to the knockout. To find the amount of SEC cable you will need, add 5 feet to the length of the chalk line.

◆ If the wall directly above the meter is less than the height required by code, you can run cable as high as possible above the meter, bend it at that point, then run it higher, parallel to the roofline *(inset)*. When you install the cable *(page 76, Step 5)*, anchor the bend with circular clamps.

CIRCULAR CLAMP

## 2. Mounting the cable clamps.

◆ Center a circular clamp over the chalk line 12 inches above the meter box and fasten the clamp to the wall with two $1\frac{1}{2}$-inch No. 8 wood screws. Drive the screws all the way in *(right)*, then unscrew them a few turns so that the clamp is loose enough for you to slide the cable under it. In a brick or concrete-block wall, mount the clamp with a drive-pin set *(page 67, Step 4)*, or use screw anchors to secure it to the wall.

◆ Mount additional clamps every 30 inches along the chalk line.

◆ At the top of the chalk line, screw the weatherhead support bracket to the wall, making sure there is enough clearance above the weatherhead to mount the insulator rack or eyebolt *(page 76, Step 4)*.

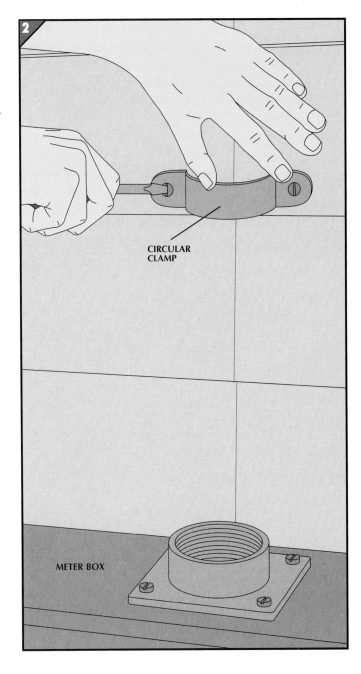

CIRCULAR CLAMP

METER BOX

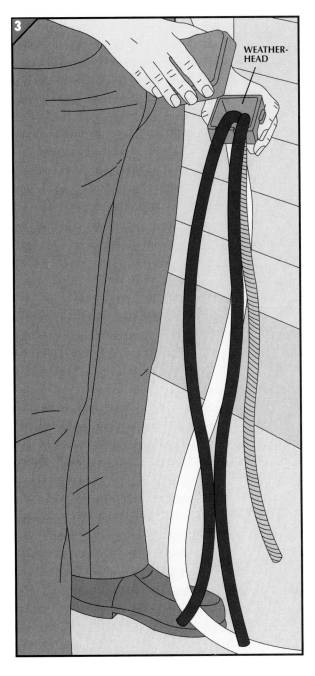

WEATHER-HEAD

## 3. Wiring the weatherhead.

◆ Strip 3 feet of sheathing from one end of the SEC cable, then twist the bare neutral wires into a single strand and bend them away from the insulated wires *(page 19)*.

◆ Remove the top of the weatherhead, thread the insulated wires through the holes in the base, and pull these wires out until the neutral wire presses against the bottom of the weatherhead.

◆ Bend the neutral against one of the unstripped cables and replace the top of the weatherhead *(left)*.

## 4. Supporting the service.

For three-wire service, fasten a three-insulator wire rack to the stud nearest the weatherhead bracket with two $\frac{3}{8}$-by-6-inch lag screws *(right)*.

If you have triplex service, secure a 2-by-4 brace next to the wall sheathing between two studs in the attic with $3\frac{1}{2}$-inch common nails, then drill a pilot hole through the brace and the siding and fasten an eyebolt to the brace *(inset)*.

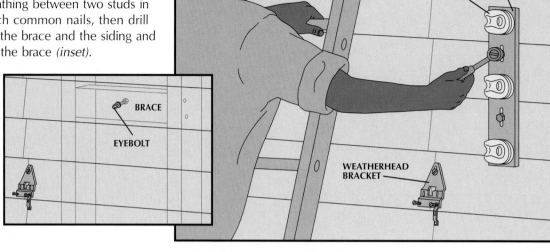

## 5. Installing the weatherhead.

◆ Slide the weatherhead into the slots of its bracket and have a helper feed the cable down through the wall clamps and into a weatherproof SEC connector *(page 68)* into the top of the meter box *(left)*.

◆ Have the helper pull the cable tight, then tighten the circular wall clamps over it.

◆ Tighten the lock nut on the weatherproof connector to fasten the cable to the meter box.

◆ Have an electrician wire the cable to the meter socket; the electric company will connect the other end of the cable to the service drop.

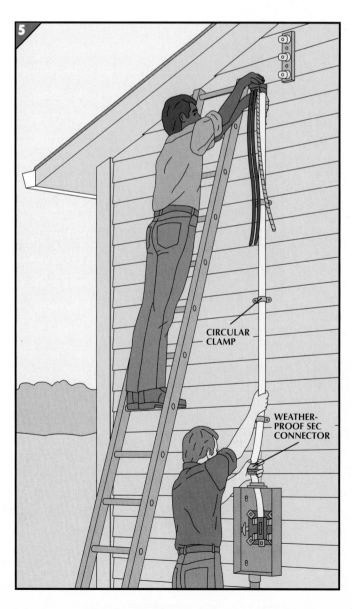

# A MAST-STYLE SERVICE ENTRANCE

EAVE

## 1. Making a hole in the roof.
◆ Drop a plumb line from the eave to the center of the meter box, mark the eave at the top of the line, and pry loose the roof shingle directly above the mark.
◆ With a hole saw $\frac{1}{2}$ inch larger than the conduit you are using as the mast, drill a hole at the mark up through the eave and roofing material *(left)*.
◆ Align the conduit on the wall and mount clamps as for a wall-mounted line *(pages 74-75, Steps 1-2)*, but use offset circular clamps and lag screws; locate one screw per clamp at a stud, if possible, and drive only one screw for now.

For a soffit, mark it as described above, remove the soffit section and cut a hole in it, using a hole saw for wood or vinyl, or tin snips for aluminum. Mark and cut the hole through the eave, then put the soffit section you removed back in place.

ROOF JACK

## 2. Weatherproofing the hole.
◆ Slide a roof jack under the loosened shingle, aligning the hole in the jack directly over the one in the roof *(above)*.

◆ Seal the jack around the hole with roofing cement, then fasten both the jack and the shingle to the roof with six $1\frac{1}{2}$-inch roofing nails.

## 3. Raising the mast.

◆ Wire the weatherhead *(page 75, Step 3)*.

◆ Have a helper on the ground push the steel conduit up through the roof jack to the mast height required by code.

◆ On the roof, slide the SEC cable down into the conduit mast *(right)* until the weatherhead rests on the top of the conduit.

◆ Have your helper attach the conduit into the meter box, then fasten the weatherhead to the mast with the setscrews located at the bottom of the head.

◆ Secure the conduit to the wall by tightening the second screw of each clamp.

◆ Screw an insulator clamp to the mast 12 inches below the weatherhead and mount the ceramic insulator on the clamp for the service drop.

## 4. Securing the mast.

If the mast rises more than 3 feet above the roof, support it with a copper or steel guy wire. To do so:

◆ Attach a circular clamp to the mast just below the weatherhead and fasten No. 6 steel or copper guy wire through two bug connectors and the clamp, as shown in the inset. Run the wire to the roof ridge in a line that is at a 90-degree angle to the wall with the meter box.

◆ Drill a $\frac{1}{4}$-inch hole in the ridge at the point where the wire crosses it and screw in a $\frac{3}{8}$-inch eyebolt with a release lever and a washer.

◆ Slip a turnbuckle into the eyebolt, open the turnbuckle by unscrewing the threaded ends, and fasten the guy wire to the loose end of the turnbuckle with a second set of bugs.

◆ Rotate the turnbuckle with pliers until the guy wire is taut *(left)*.

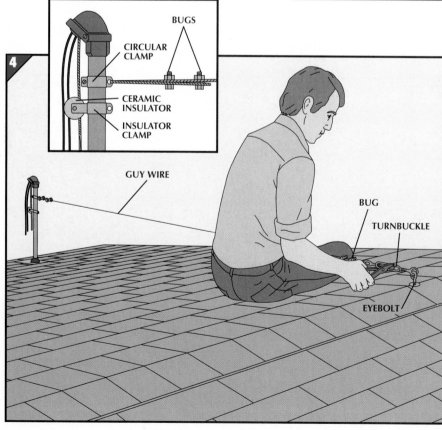

# An Underground Power Line

Sheltered from the elements, underground lines are a practical alternative to an overhead service.

**Underground Cable:** Underground Service Entrance (USE) and Underground Feeder (UF) cables, both sheathed in plastic, are sturdy enough to be laid directly in a trench, without conduit. And although a short trench still must be dug with a shovel, tool-rental companies can supply you with a power trenching machine for a long one. If you replace a main overhead service with an underground cable, the part of the cable that goes aboveground to your meter must be encased in conduit.

**Planning the Project:** If you plan to convert a main overhead service

to an underground one, discuss your plan with the electric company; many companies will pay for the trenches, the cable, or both. Even if your company does not, it will help you map a route for your trench and make the final connection at the pole.

**Code Requirements:** The National Electrical Code specifies many details of an underground installation. USE and UF cables must be 24 inches below grade for a service or circuit that is more than 30 amperes, 12 inches below grade for one that is less. Under driveways, patios, or sidewalks, the cable must be encased in galvanized-steel conduit. In extremely rocky soil, the cable must lie on a 3-inch bed of sand and be covered by 3 or more

inches of sand. The protection of the sand is worth having even when it is not required; if you want it, dig a trench 3 inches below the code specification to put the cable at the right depth. Finally, check local building code; some codes call for a support of drain tile, wood, or concrete in addition to sand.

> **⚠ CAUTION** *Never work near a live service drop while you set up an underground service—have the electric company cut off power.*

> **⚠ CAUTION** *Before excavating a trench, locate underground obstacles such as dry wells, septic tanks, and cesspools, and electric, water, and sewer lines.*

 **TOOLS**

Chalk line
Trenching machine

Square-edged shovel
Maul
Half-round file

 **MATERIALS**

Polyethylene sheeting
Sand
Electrical cable

Galvanized-steel conduit and fittings
Sealing compound
Patching concrete

**SAFETY TIPS**

*Goggles protect your eyes when you are hammering steel conduit.*

## 1. Removing the sod.

◆ Mark the path of the trench on the ground by snapping two parallel chalk lines 8 inches apart, and lay a sheet of plastic film along one side of the planned path.

◆ Loosen the sod within the lines with a square-edged shovel *(right)*, then divide the loosened sod into 2-foot sections and lift them onto the plastic with the shovel.

◆ At the edge of a driveway, sidewalk, or patio, broaden the trench to make room to drive conduit *(page 80, Step 3)*.

## 2. Digging the trench.

◆ Set a trenching machine at one end of the trench path with its digging teeth poised above the ground, adjust the drive speed for your soil according to the manufacturer's instructions, and start the motor.

◆ For the model shown here, release a clutch next to the handle to start the teeth rotating, then turn the height-adjustment wheel on the body to lower them to the trench depth you have chosen.

◆ Engage the drive release to move the machine backward, and guide it by the handles at the rear *(right)*. If there is a large rock along the trench path, stop the machine, move it beyond the rock, and continue trenching. Remove the rock later or, if it is too difficult to move, reroute the trench around it.

◆ Lay a bed of sand 3 inches deep at the bottom of the trench.

DRIVE RELEASE

HEIGHT-ADJUSTMENT WHEEL

GALVANIZED-STEEL CONDUIT

WOOD BLOCK

## 3. Running conduit and cable.

◆ For an obstruction such as a driveway or sidewalk, cut a length of galvanized-steel conduit 1 foot longer than the obstruction. Cover the leading end of the conduit with a closed plastic bushing.

◆ Supporting the conduit at the correct height on wood blocks, drive it with a maul *(left)* until it extends at least 6 inches beyond the obstruction.

◆ Remove the burrs from the cut end of the conduit with a half-round file *(page 71, Step 2)*, and the bushing from the leading end.

◆ Cover each end with a setscrew connector and an open bushing.

◆ Lay cable in the trench and push it through the conduit. In the trench, bend the cable at 18-inch intervals to form a zigzag pattern, which will prevent the cable from becoming overly taut should settling occur.

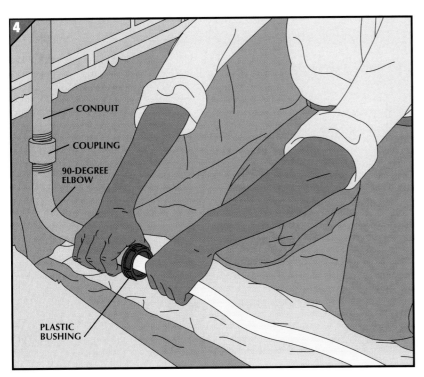

CONDUIT

COUPLING

90-DEGREE
ELBOW

PLASTIC
BUSHING

## 4. Completing the service.

◆ Cut a length of conduit to reach from the bottom of the meter box to the middle of the trench, then connect it to the meter with a setscrew terminal adapter and a grounding lock nut *(page 69)*.

◆ Attach a 90-degree galvanized-steel elbow to the conduit with a coupling, and fasten a plastic bushing to the elbow.

◆ Feed the cable into the elbow *(left)*, up the conduit, and into the meter box.

◆ Waterproof the underground elbow opening with sealing compound.

◆ Run cable from the meter to the service panel through the house wall *(page 63, Step 2)*.

◆ Cover the cable in the trench with a 3-inch layer of sand, shovel in 4 inches of dirt, and compact the dirt with a 4-by-4. Continue adding 4-inch layers of compacted dirt until the trench is almost full, then replace the sod.

### TRICKS OF THE TRADE

### Protecting Underground Cable

Codes specifying how deep to bury underground cable are designed to safeguard it from damage during later excavations, but you can provide additional protection with plastic pipe. After laying the cable in its trench, lay lengths of PVC or ABS piping on top of it, then backfill the trench as described above. Should anyone dig in the area, the shovel will strike the pipe before it reaches the cable, shielding the wiring from damage and providing a warning to dig elsewhere.

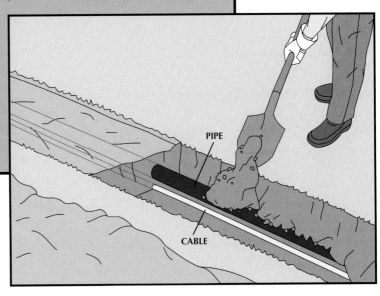

PIPE

CABLE

# 3 Wiring for Communication

For many of their functions, televisions, stereos, and telephones routinely use levels of electricity that are lower than the 120 volts supplied by the power company. The low-voltage wiring for these systems can be routed practically anywhere inside or outside the house more simply and safely than high-voltage cables. Working with it requires a few specialized tools and supplies.

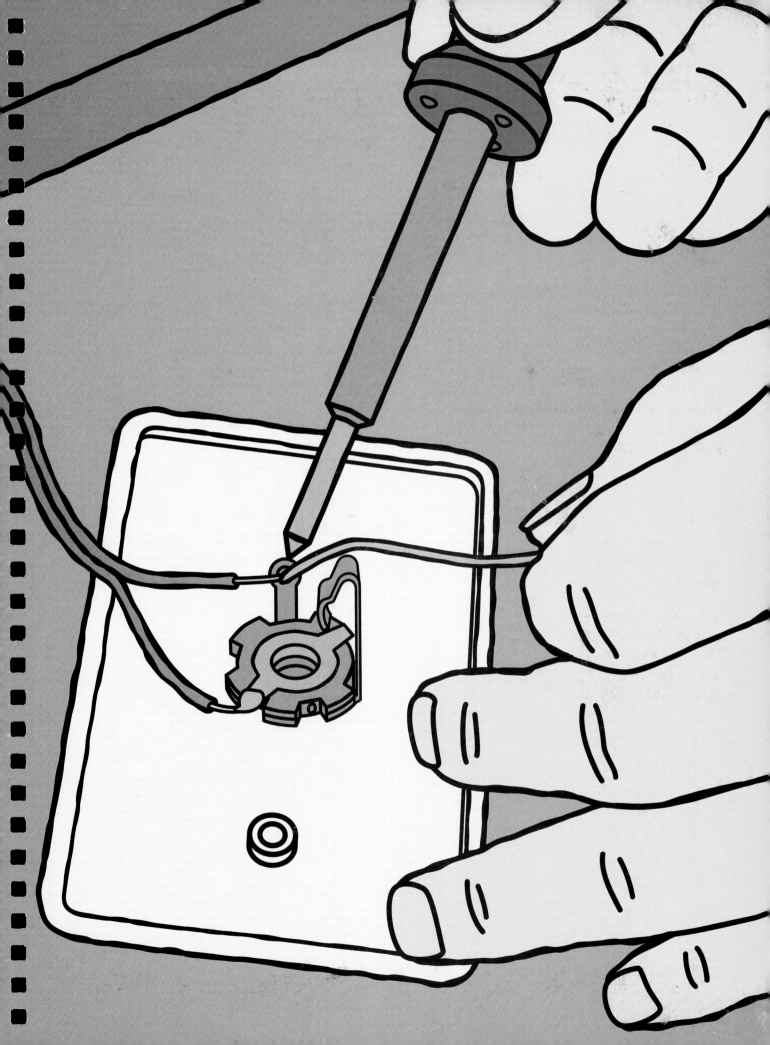

# Low-Voltage Wires: Easy to Connect and Conceal

**W**ires for circuits of 30 volts or less are generally smaller, lighter, and more flexible than regular 120- or 240-volt house wiring, and are easier to handle. Since they present little or no hazard, they are subject to few code regulations, so you can install them almost any way you please. Because they may carry not only power but also complex signals for television sets, speakers, and telephones, they come in a variety of shapes and colors *(below)* to facilitate connections.

**Routing Cable:** You can hide low-voltage wires in the same places as high-voltage cables *(pages 10-17)* so long as you keep the two types at least 2 inches apart. You can also take advantage of routes prohibited for high-voltage wires, such as the places shown on pages 86 and 87. Where their appearance is not obtrusive, fasten the wires directly to walls. Low-voltage wires also lend themselves to a variety of easy fishing and fastening techniques *(opposite)*.

Do not run wire where it could be damaged by foot traffic or furniture. If you run cable outdoors, use wires rated for resistance to moisture, heat, and stress. Route television and stereo cables in gentle curves; sharp bends can alter the electrical properties of the wire and hasten deterioration of the insulation.

**Making Connections:** The wires can be joined almost anywhere, without a junction box. Small wire caps and screw terminals will serve for most connections, although some should be soldered *(pages 91-94)*. You can also use a variety of connectors that can be crimped onto the ends of wires *(pages 88-89)*; the insulation on the sleeve of a crimp connector is color-coded for wire sizes—red is for Nos. 22 to 18 gauge, blue for Nos. 16 to 14. In addition, several specialized connectors are made for the cables that interconnect stereo components and join television sets to satellite-dish or antenna systems.

 *Connect low-voltage wires carefully—even at low* **CAUTION** *voltages, sparks from a loose connection could cause a fire.*

---

 **TOOLS**

| | | | |
|---|---|---|---|
| Screwdriver | Crochet hook | Coax-cable | |
| Pry bar | Diagonal cutters | crimper | |
| Staple gun | Utility knife | Pliers | Soldering iron |
| Electric drill | Chisel | Multipurpose | Long-nose |
| Fish tape | Mallet | tool | pliers |

**MATERIALS**

| | | |
|---|---|---|
| | Coax cable clips | F-connectors |
| | Cable clamps | Pin plugs |
| Low-voltage cable | Silicone caulking | Solder |
| Staples | Crimp connectors | Heat-shrink |
| Thumbtacks | Quick connectors | tubing |

---

## AN ARRAY OF WIRES AND CABLES

The most commonly used type of low-voltage wire is called bell wire or hookup wire. It comes in single strands or in multiple-conductor cables containing from two to several dozen color-coded wires that are twisted together and encased in a plastic jacket. Ordinary lamp cord, known as zip cord, since it can be separated, or zipped, along a groove in the insulation, is also used on low-voltage circuits. The coding may be by ridges or stripes on the insulation or by color or a colored thread in the stranded wire. Audio-coax cable is used for wiring stereo components other than speakers. It consists of a series of concentric sheaths around a stranded center conductor: a ring of foam insulation, a second ring of twisted or braided outer conductor, and an outer ring of insulation. TV coax cable—for connecting TVs to antennas or satellite dishes—is similar, but has a solid center conductor, thicker inner insulation—often plastic foam—and a weatherproof outer insulation. In both types, the braided wire forms a shield to protect the conductor from interference. Flat twin-lead, used for indoor FM antennas, has two conductors set about $\frac{1}{4}$ inch apart in plastic insulation. Shielded twin-lead, an improved version, has two foam-insulated wires in foil sheathing and is protected by an outer layer of plastic insulation.

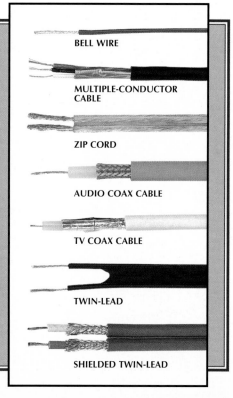

BELL WIRE

MULTIPLE-CONDUCTOR CABLE

ZIP CORD

AUDIO COAX CABLE

TV COAX CABLE

TWIN-LEAD

SHIELDED TWIN-LEAD

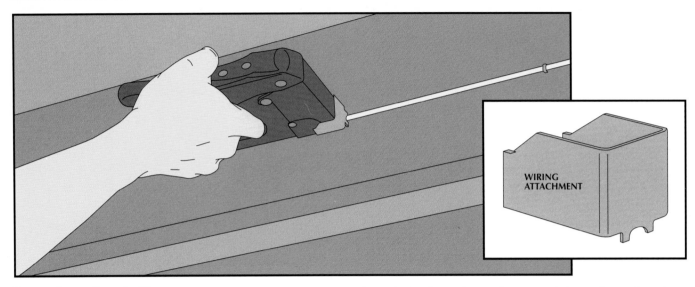

### Fastening wires in the open.

To fasten bell wire, jacketed cable, or zip cord to joists, baseboards, or moldings, first center a staple gun fitted with a slip-on wiring attachment *(inset)* over the wire, straddling it, and hold the gun lightly against the wire so that you do not crush its insulation. Squeeze the handle to drive a staple *(above)*. Space the staples close enough together so the wiring does not sag.

For twin-lead, set the staple gun at right angles to the wires and staple into the insulation between conductors.

Fasten coax cable with special clips *(page 108, Step 4)*.

Secure shielded twin-lead and jacketed cables too large for staples or clips with the cable clamps or staples normally used for high-voltage cables.

### Fishing wires between floors.

◆ Next to a baseboard on the upper floor, drill a hole down into the space between the floor joists.
◆ Feed a length of heavy string, secured by a nail or furniture leg, into the hole.
◆ From the lower room or a closet, drill a hole into the same joist space.
◆ Feed a fish tape through the hole toward the string and twist the tape to snag the string *(left)* and pull it down through the hole
◆ Tie the wire to the string and pull the wire to the upper floor.

# HIDING WIRES

### A houseful of wires.

The cutaway house at right contains more low-voltage wires, in more places, than any house is likely to have—but it shows many of the ways such wiring can be completely hidden, or how wires can simply be stapled to a wall as inconspicuously as possible. In many cases, wires can simply be routed along closet walls or through holes drilled in a floor.

### Outside the house.

If you cannot conveniently route low-voltage wires indoors, you can run them outdoors and then back into the house.

◆ Drill a small hole through the house wall just above the foundation.

◆ Run the wire through the hole and staple it *(page 85)* along the underside of the siding, as shown above.

◆ Drill a second hole in the wall or through a window frame and run the wire back inside.

◆ Seal each hole with silicone caulking.

### Along molding.
Tuck the wire into the space between the ceiling and the molding at the top of a wall *(left)*, securing it at corners with broad-headed thumb tacks.

Alternatively, staple wire to the underside of chair rail—a type of molding generally installed about 36 inches off the floor.

### Behind trim.
◆ With a utility knife, slit the paint seal where a baseboard or door casing meets the wall.
◆ Pry the trim loose with a chisel and a mallet.
◆ Run wire in the gap between the wallboard and the floor. In a plaster wall, chisel a groove for the wire.
◆ Replace the baseboard carefully, angling any new nails to miss the wire.

### At the edge of a carpet.
Poke the wire down into the space between the bottom of a wall and the edge of a carpet. If the carpet is too thin to conceal the wire, use a crochet hook to pull the edge of the carpet away from the wall slightly, tuck the wire under the edge, and smooth the carpet back into place.

### At a doorway.
Pry up or unscrew the edging strip that covers the joint between two types of flooring, staple the wire along the edge, and replace the strip. Take special care not to drive nails or screws through the wire.

# PREPARING CABLES FOR THEIR CONNECTIONS

### Stripping multiconductor cable.

◆ Cut a short lengthwise slit at the end of the sheathing with an electrician's knife.

◆ Hold the slit end of the sheathing—but not the wires—with a pair of pliers, and pull one of the wires out from the slit with a second pair, tearing the sheathing *(right)*.

◆ Snip off the torn sheathing and strip the individual wires *(page 19)*.

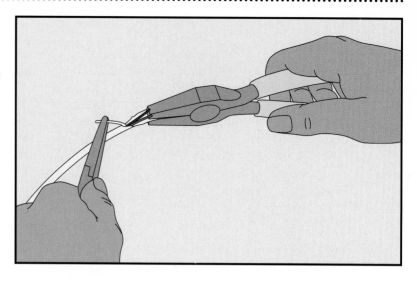

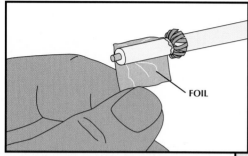

FOIL

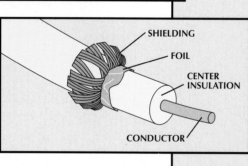

SHIELDING

FOIL

CENTER INSULATION

CONDUCTOR

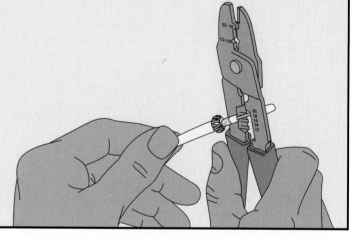

### Stripping TV coax cable.

◆ Remove $\frac{3}{4}$ inch of the outer cable sheathing with a multipurpose tool.

◆ Pull the braided shielding wires away from the center insulation, trim them to $\frac{1}{4}$ inch, and fold the ends back over the edge of the sheathing. If the cable has a loose foil shield between the shielding and the insulation, peel it off *(top inset)*. If foil is bonded to the insulation, do not disturb it.

◆ With the 16-gauge setting on the multipurpose tool, strip $\frac{3}{8}$ inch of the insulation and any bonded foil *(above)*, exposing the inner conductor *(bottom inset)*.

---

## A SPECIAL TV COAX-CABLE STRIPPER

When you have a lot of TV coax cable to strip, you can get the job done quickly with a special tool made for the purpose. With its two blades, the TV coax-cable stripper cuts the outer sheathing, shielding wires, and center insulation to the appropriate length in one operation. Simply squeeze the handles of the stripper, slip the cable between its jaws with the longer blade $\frac{3}{8}$ inch from the end, then close the jaws and rotate the tool a full turn. The first blade severs the sheathing while the second cuts the shielding and insulation. To remove the insulation and expose the inner conductor, pull the stripper away from the cable.

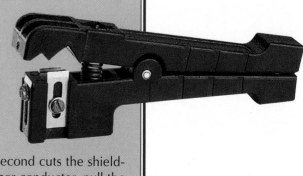

# CRIMPING ON CONNECTORS

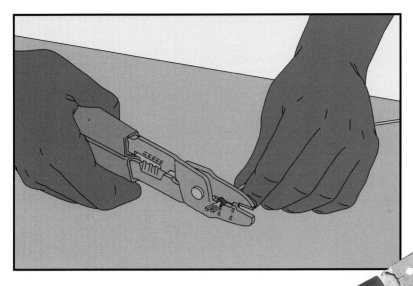

### Installing crimp connectors.
◆ Strip $\frac{1}{4}$ inch of insulation from a wire *(page 19)* and slip a connector, color-coded for the wire size *(page 84)*, over the bare wire end.
◆ Crush the sleeve of the connector onto the wire with the matching, number-coded crimping die of a multipurpose tool *(left)*.
◆ Attach lugs for screw terminals, as well as male and female quick connectors *(photograph)*, in the same way.

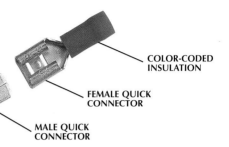

COLOR-CODED INSULATION

FEMALE QUICK CONNECTOR

MALE QUICK CONNECTOR

### Installing a TV coax-cable connector.
◆ Strip the cable *(opposite)*, then slip the metal collar, or ferrule, supplied with the appropriate coax-cable connector over the stripped end.
◆ Push the connector over the center insulation so the tapered neck of the connector slips under the braided shielding *(right, top)*, and is completely covered, and the braiding fits snugly against the back of the connector.
◆ Slide the ferrule over the neck and crimp it firmly with a coax-cable crimper/cutter *(right, bottom)* or long-nose pliers to secure it to the cable.

For audio coax cable, solder both inner and outer conductors to a pin plug *(pages 93-94)*.

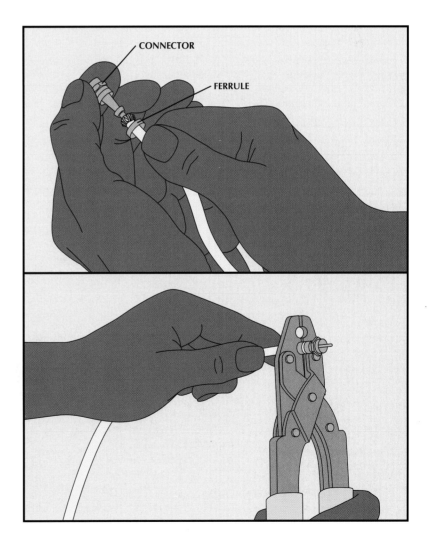

CONNECTOR

FERRULE

# SPLICING WITH A TIGHT-FITTING TUBE

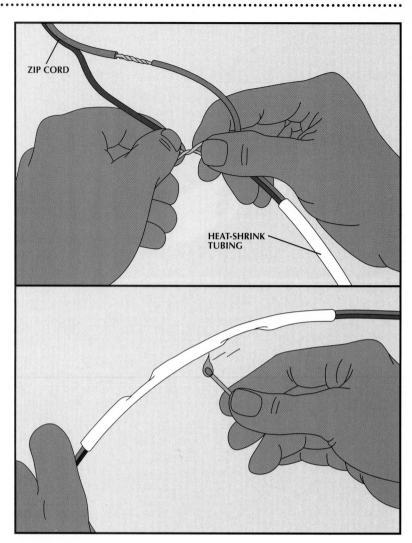

ZIP CORD

HEAT-SHRINK TUBING

### Using heat-shrink tubing.

When it is necessary to splice two lengths of low-voltage wiring, use a soldered joint protected by heat-shrink tubing. The tubing is available at electronics stores in widths that match most wires. Avoid splices unless there is no other way to run a length of wire from one point to another.

◆ To prepare the two wires—in this case zip cord—for splicing, slip a 6-inch length of $\frac{1}{4}$-inch tubing over the cord and separate about 4 inches of the conductors in each of the two cords.

◆ Offset the splices by cutting 2 inches from the copper wire of one cord and from the silver wire of the other.

◆ Strip 1 inch of insulation from all four conductors *(page 19)*, then twist the two silver wires and the two copper wires together *(right, top)*.

◆ Solder each connection *(opposite)*.

◆ Slide the tubing over both splices and hold a match or lighter just under it *(right, bottom)*, moving the flame rapidly back to shrink the tubing.

### TRICKS OF THE TRADE

#### Splicing TV Coax Cable

Instead of replacing an entire run of damaged TV coax cable, you can remove the damaged section and splice the wiring together with special connectors. First, cut away the damage with wire cutters, strip both cut ends *(page 88)*, and attach an F-connector to each one *(page 89)*. Screw a barrel connector onto one F-connector, then secure the other to the barrel connector.

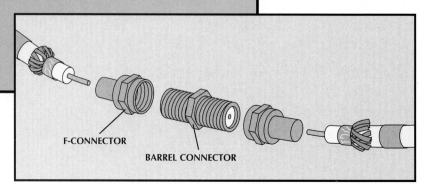

F-CONNECTOR

BARREL CONNECTOR

# The Simple Art of Soldering

To guarantee mechanically secure, electrically correct connections in many low-voltage circuits, wires can be soldered to flat metal tabs or inside the cylindrical prongs of pin plugs. For these jobs, you need a soldering iron, consisting of a pencil-thin metal bar with a concealed heating element and a heatproof handle; a 25- to 50-watt element is adequate for connecting most low-voltage wires.

**Electrical Solder:** An easy-melting wire of tin and lead with a chemical core to aid bonding, electrical solder comes in several varieties. Use rosin-core solder for all electrical work—never use acid-core solder, which looks somewhat similar but is designed for plumbing and heavy metal work and can corrode small wires. The rosin core, called flux, acts as a high-temperature cleaning agent, preventing oxides from forming on metal as it is heated.

**Techniques:** Dirt, including oxides, is the cause of most soldering problems. Use a file, a stiff wire brush, or a scrap of sandpaper to clean the tip of the iron before you begin to solder. Keep a clean, damp sponge nearby and dab the tip of the iron on it frequently to remove foreign matter. Also thoroughly clean all surfaces that are to be soldered; if possible, bring the surface to a shine. Provide good light and place your work so that you can see the connection clearly.

After dirt, the principal fault in soldering is uneven heating. To avoid this problem, always heat the larger piece in a connection, letting it conduct heat to the smaller. Never heat the solder directly; hot solder dripping onto a cold surface creates a poor bond, or none at all.

⚠ **CAUTION** *Place a small wood pad under the work to prevent burning the work surface, and never leave a plugged-in iron unattended.*

### TOOLS

Soldering iron
Soldering gun
Soldering stand
File, wire brush,
   or sandpaper
Sponge
Long-nose pliers
Multipurpose tool

### MATERIALS

Solder
Wood pad
Low-voltage cable
Adapter plate
Nail
Pin plugs

## CONNECTING WIRE TO A TERMINAL

### 1. Tinning the iron.

◆ Heat the soldering iron. A soldering gun *(photograph)*, generally fitted with an adjustable trigger that controls the temperature of the tip, heats the work more quickly; it is comparatively expensive but worth the extra money if you do a good deal of precision soldering.

◆ Dab a small amount of solder directly onto the tip of the iron with a brushing motion, then wipe the tip clean on a sponge or moist cloth and reapply a small amount of solder *(right)*.

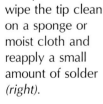

SOLDERING
GUN

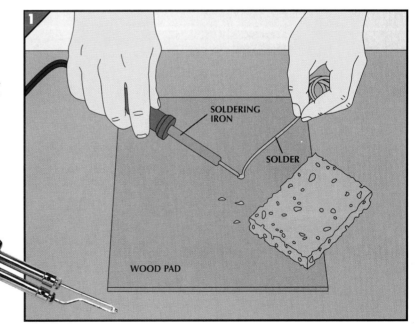

SOLDERING IRON

SOLDER

WOOD PAD

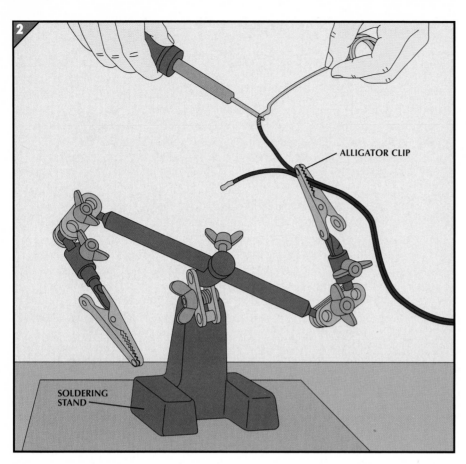

ALLIGATOR CLIP

SOLDERING STAND

## 2. Tinning the leads.

◆ Prepare the wires—in this example, zip cord—by separating about 4 inches of the conductors and stripping $1\frac{1}{2}$ inches of insulation from both wires (page 19).

◆ Twist the stripped strands of wire together and secure the cord in one of the alligator clips of a soldering stand.

◆ Heat one of the wire ends with a soldering iron and apply a small amount of solder to the wire—not the iron. If the wire is hot enough, the solder will melt almost instantly and coat the wire evenly. If the solder does not melt, heat the wire a little longer and try again.

◆ Apply solder to the other wire end in the same way (left).

### TRICKS OF THE TRADE

### Holding Wires Steady

If you don't have a special stand to support wires while you are soldering, you can use a weight such as a pair of pliers to hold wiring steady and elevated from the work surface. Simply set the wire on the surface, make a bend in it about 6 inches from the end, and place the weight on the bend.

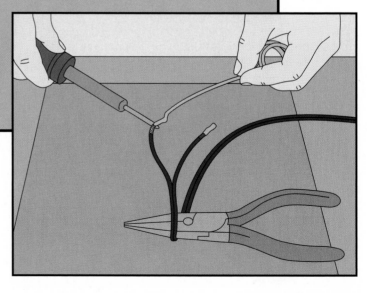

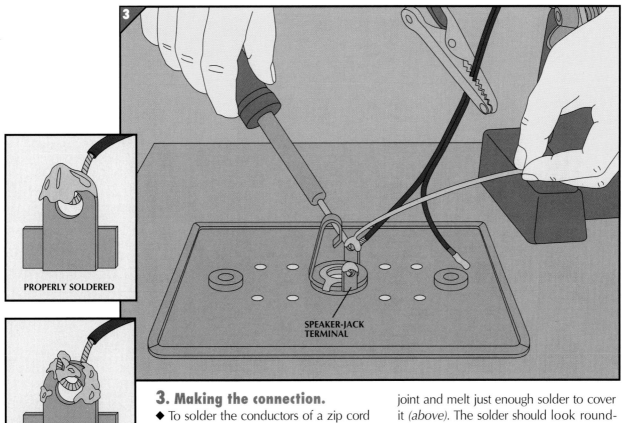

PROPERLY SOLDERED

IMPROPERLY SOLDERED

SPEAKER-JACK
TERMINAL

### 3. Making the connection.

◆ To solder the conductors of a zip cord to the terminals of a speaker jack *(page 97, Step 2)*, pull one wire through a terminal tab with long-nose pliers and wrap it tightly in a loop around the tab.

◆ Press the tip of the soldering iron to the underside of the joint. When the joint is heated, touch the solder to the joint and melt just enough solder to cover it *(above)*. The solder should look rounded and smooth *(top inset)*. If it is uneven and lumpy *(bottom inset)*, reheat the joint; usually reheating will distribute the solder properly, making it unnecessary for you to add more.

◆ Solder the second wire to the remaining terminal in the same way.

# ATTACHING A PIN PLUG

### 1. Preparing the leads.

◆ Prepare the wiring—in this example, zipped audio coax cable—by separating about 4 inches of the conductors and stripping $1\frac{1}{2}$ inches of the outer insulation. Then, using the point of a nail, tease apart the braided or spiral ground wire that surrounds one of the insulated positive leads.

◆ Twist the ground wire tightly to form a lead and strip $\frac{3}{4}$ inch of the foam insulation sheathing the positive lead.

◆ Prepare the second wire in the same manner *(right)*.

◆ Tin the soldering iron and both leads *(pages 91-92, Steps 1-2)* and trim the ground lead to a length of $\frac{1}{8}$ inch.

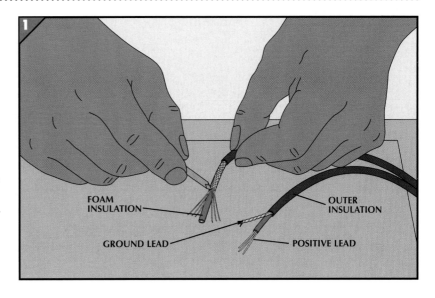

FOAM
INSULATION

OUTER
INSULATION

GROUND LEAD

POSITIVE LEAD

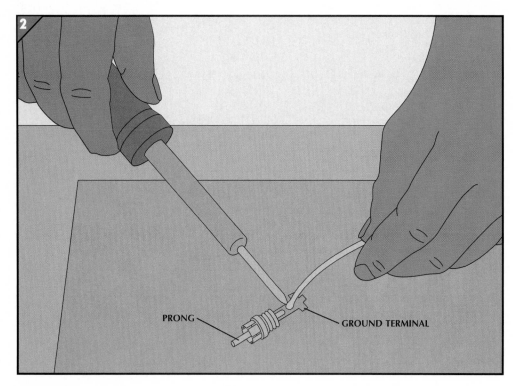

**2. Preparing the plug.**

◆ For each conductor, heat the ground terminal at the back of a pin plug, and melt a drop of solder onto it about $\frac{1}{4}$ inch from the end *(left)*.

◆ Push the cap of the plug over the stripped wire, and poke the wire through the plug so that the positive lead protrudes through the end of the prong.

PRONG

GROUND TERMINAL

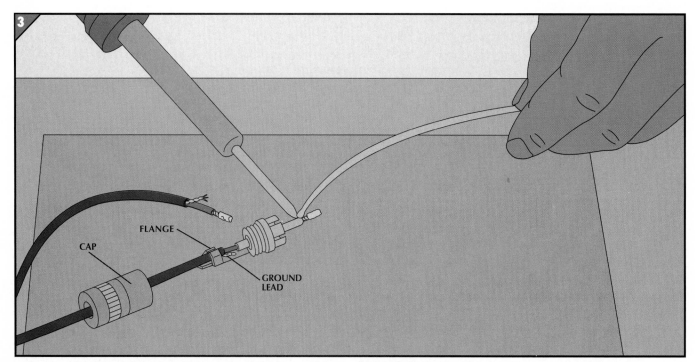

FLANGE

CAP

GROUND LEAD

**3. Securing the plug.**

◆ Aligning the plug so the ground lead lies on the solder dot on the ground terminal, pinch the ground terminal flanges around the cable with long-nose pliers, then heat the prong of the plug.

◆ Apply solder so it flows down the wire inside and closes the tip opening *(above)*.

◆ Cut off the excess wire and use the hot iron wire to wipe away any solder that has congealed on the plug.

◆ Place the iron under the ground terminal to melt the dot of solder and bond the ground lead.

◆ Screw on the cap.

Incorporating additional components to the standard elements of a stereo sound system, you can install remote speakers, volume controls, and headphone outlets to custom-design a system for your house.

**Installing Remote Speakers:**
Almost every amplifier has an extra set of terminals for a second pair of speakers at a remote location. Where space is at a premium, you can mount speakers in the ceiling *(page 96)*.

Some amplifiers have terminals for two sets of remote speakers, but few amplifiers can drive more than two sets simultaneously—normally, one main set and one remote—without a risk of overload and damage. For three pairs of speakers, you can use a multiple-speaker switch box, available at electronics parts stores, to protect the amplifier. With four or more pairs, you will need a distribution system such as the one on pages 101 to 103. Separate volume controls for remote speakers *(page 96)* enable you to alter their volume without returning to the amplifier.

A set of permanently installed outlets *(page 97)* will allow you to plug and unplug speakers to move them from room to room or from indoors to outdoors. Outdoor outlets *(page 100)* must be protected by the type of weatherproof enclosure normally used for 120-volt receptacles, but for a permanent outdoor installation, you can wire weatherproof speakers in exactly the same way as those indoors, or install recessed speakers in a protected location.

For wire runs of 60 feet or less, use No. 18 cable; longer runs require No. 16.

**Headphone Outlets:** For private indoor listening at a remote location, use a wall-mounted headphone outlet with its own volume control *(pages 98-99)*. Because headphones require less power than speakers, you can connect up to 12 outlets to one amplifier.

 **TOOLS**

Multipurpose tool
Wire cutters
Screwdriver
Keyhole saw

Electric drill
Soldering Iron
Fish tape
Continuity tester
Hammer
Tin snips

 **MATERIALS**

Low-voltage cable (two-
 and three-conductor)
Remote volume control
Wire caps
Recessed stereo speakers
Screw anchors

Solderless connectors
Headphone plugs ($\frac{1}{4}$")
Solder
Wall plate
Double-gang switch plate
Headphone jack
Jumper wires
Resistors (330-ohm, 2-watt)

Steel pipe ($\frac{1}{2}$")
Tee fitting
Outdoor electrical box,
 cover, and gasket
Outdoor receptacle
Scrap lumber
Machine screws (1")
Switch plate

# HOOKUPS AND CONTROLS FOR REMOTE SPEAKERS

**Connecting remote speakers.**
◆ Run coded two-conductor cables *(pages 85-87)* between the amplifier and the remote speakers.
◆ Strip $\frac{1}{2}$ inch of insulation from the end of each conductor, and tin the ends *(page 92, Step 2)*.
◆ At the back of the amplifier, attach the wires to the remote-speaker terminals. The connections may be made with screws *(inset, top)*, spring-loaded clamps, spade lugs, or pin plugs. To the left positive terminal, attach the conductor that will run to the left speaker's positive terminal; and to the left negative terminal, secure the conductor for the left speaker's negative terminal. Attach the right-speaker wires to the right terminals in a similar manner.
◆ At each speaker, match the wires to their terminals *(inset, bottom)*.

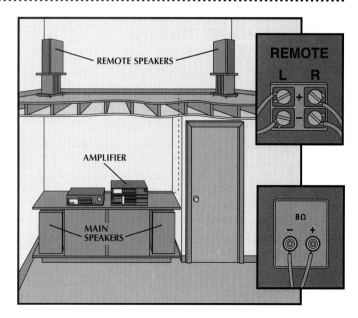

## Wiring a remote volume control.

◆ In a wall near the speakers, cut a rectangular hole *(page 15, Step 1)* 2 by 2½ inches for an auto-transformer-type volume control.

◆ From the hole, run three-conductor cable to the amplifier and a coded two-conductor speaker cable to each speaker.

◆ At the amplifier's remote-speaker terminals, connect the red wire of the three-conductor cable to the right positive terminal, the white wire to the left positive terminal, and the black wire to the left negative terminal. Attach the two-conductor cable wires to the speaker terminals *(page 95)*.

◆ Working on the volume control *(inset)*, on the side marked input, connect the white wire from the amplifier to input terminal 1 and the red wire to input terminal 2. With a wire cap, connect the black wire to the two black leads attached to the input side of the control. On the output side of the control—located opposite the input side—fasten the positive wire of the left speaker to terminal 1, the positive wire of the right speaker to terminal 2, and the negative wire from each speaker to the corresponding black output lead.

◆ Screw the control's faceplate to brackets in the wall hole *(page 116)*.

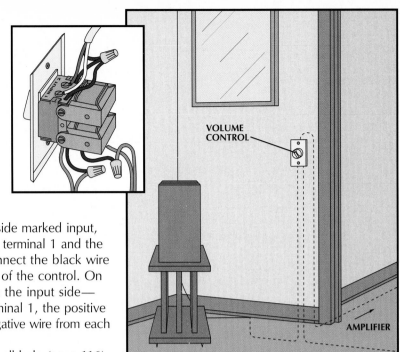

# A CEILING-MOUNTED SPEAKER

### 1. Installing the enclosure.

◆ Between two ceiling joists, cut a hole *(page 15, Step 1)* the size of the speaker enclosure.

◆ Set the enclosure in the hole and mark the positions of the flange holes on the ceiling *(left)*.

◆ Remove the enclosure, drill a pilot hole at each mark, and install anchors for the screws supplied into every second hole.

◆ From the amplifier, fish two-conductor wire through the enclosure hole *(pages 85-87)*, thread it through a knockout in the enclosure, and screw the enclosure to the anchors.

### 2. Wiring the speaker.

◆ With a solderless connector *(page 89)*, attach the positive speaker wire to the positive speaker terminal, indicated by a red dot or a plus sign on the speaker frame *(right)*. Join the negative wire to the second terminal.

◆ Screw the speaker flange to the mounting holes in the enclosure flange.

◆ Install a second recessed speaker in the same way.

◆ Connect both speakers to an amplifier or remote volume control.

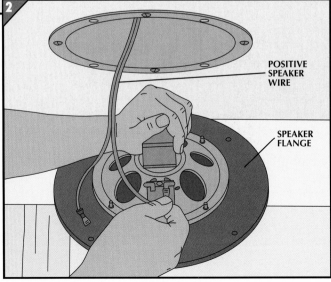

# PLUGS FOR PORTABILITY

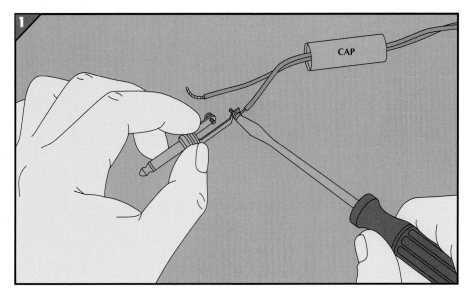

## 1. Wiring a speaker plug.
◆ Slip the cap of a $\frac{1}{4}$-inch headphone plug over a No. 18 two-conductor coded cable, and cut the silver conductor $\frac{1}{2}$ inch shorter than the copper one.
◆ Tin the ends of both wires (page 92, Step 2), then attach the copper wire to the long screw terminal of the plug (left).
◆ Fasten the copper wire to the short terminal, then screw the cap onto the plug.
◆ Attach the other end of the cable to a speaker (page 95).

## 2. Wiring a speaker outlet.
◆ At a convenient location for a speaker, drill a 1-inch hole in the wall.
◆ Fish speaker cable from an amplifier or remote volume control (pages 95-96) out through the hole.
◆ Tin the ends of both wires, then solder the conductors to the terminals of a speaker jack mounted on a wall plate, connecting the silver conductor to the sleeve contact and the copper conductor to the spring contact (right).
◆ Insert the jack in the hole and screw the plate to the wall.

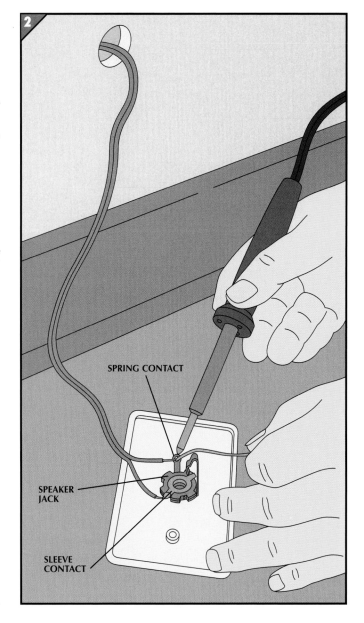

SPRING CONTACT

SPEAKER JACK

SLEEVE CONTACT

# ADDING EARPHONES

## 1. Assembling the wall plate.

You can mount a volume control with a jack for headphones by modifying a standard blank double-gang switch plate.

◆ Drill two $\frac{3}{8}$-inch holes midway between the upper and lower screw holes in the plate, and slide the shaft of a stereo L-pad volume control through one hole from the back.

◆ Slip the marked dial over the shaft, fasten it with a nut and washer *(right)*, and slip on the knob.

◆ Fasten a three-conductor stereo headphone jack into the other hole.

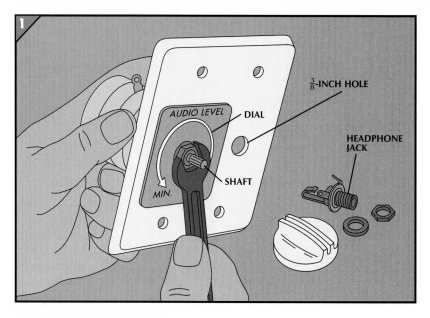

## 2. Soldering jumpers to the control.

Solder 4-inch jumper wires to three terminals of the volume control *(pages 91-94)*: Attach a black wire to the No. 1 terminal next to the mounting plate *(left)*, a white wire to the No. 2 terminal next to the plate, and a red wire to the remaining No. 2 terminal.

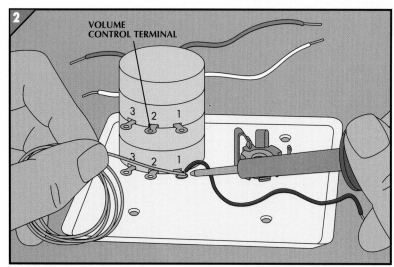

## 3. Linking the control and the jack.

◆ With a continuity tester, determine the connections between the jack's terminals and its three spring contacts: Snap the tester's clip onto the short spring contact and touch the probe to each terminal in turn *(right)* until the bulb lights. Label that terminal as "s" for short.

◆ Match and label the terminal that matches the long spring contact.

◆ Solder the red jumper from the control to the terminal for the short spring contact, the white jumper to the terminal for the long spring contact, and the black jumper to the remaining terminal for the sleeve contact.

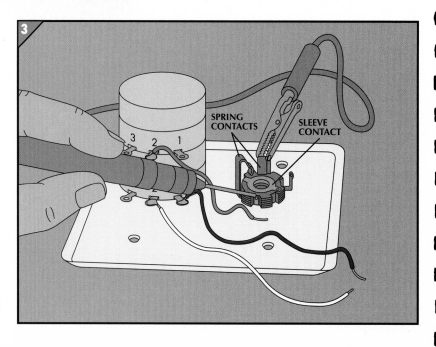

## 4. Wiring the volume control.

◆ Strip 3 inches of sheathing at one end of a 12-inch length of three-conductor cable *(page 18)*, trim the red wire by about 1 inch, then strip $1\frac{1}{2}$ inches of insulation from the black conductor, and $\frac{1}{2}$ inch of insulation from the white and red conductors *(page 19)*.

◆ Solder the white wire to the No. 3 terminal next to the plate and the red wire to the No. 3 terminal of the volume control.

◆ Feed the bare black wire through the unused No. 1 terminal of the volume control onto the No. 1 plate terminal, loop the end of the wire around this terminal, and solder the wire at each terminal *(right)*, taking care not to disconnect the jumper already connected to the No. 1 plate terminal.

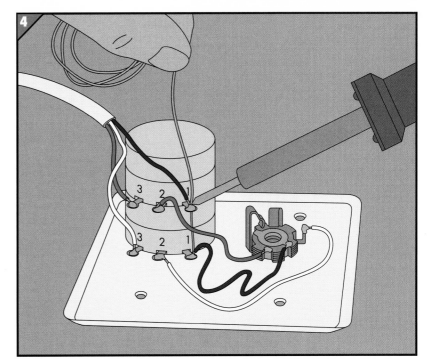

## 5. Completing the connections.

◆ At the desired location, cut a wall opening *(page 15, Step 1)* $2\frac{1}{2}$ inches high and 4 inches wide for the volume control/jack assembly.

◆ Fish three-conductor cable from the amplifier to the opening *(pages 85-87)* and, with wire caps, connect the cable wires to the matching wires of the control cable.

◆ Screw the control assembly into the wall.

◆ At the amplifier *(inset)*, use wire caps to attach 330-ohm, 2-watt resistors to the red and white wires of the three-conductor cable, and fasten the resistors to the left and right positive amplifier terminals and the black wire to the left negative terminal.

Use separate resistors for each additional headphone outlet.

# TAKING SOUND OUT OF DOORS

## 1. Installing an outlet box.
◆ Join 6- and 12-inch lengths of $\frac{1}{2}$-inch steel pipe with a T-fitting, then fasten the free end of the 6-inch length into the bottom knockout of an outdoor electrical box.

◆ Dig a foot-wide, 4-inch-deep hole at the planned speaker location and, protecting the box with scrap lumber, hammer the assembly into the hole *(right)* until the T is at the bottom, facing in the direction you plan to run the cable.

◆ Dig a 4-inch-deep trench between the box and the house *(page 80, Step 2)*, and drill a hole through the house wall above the trench *(page 86)*.

◆ Run three-conductor cable through the hole to the indoor amplifier *(pages 85 and 96)*.

◆ Outside, lay the cable in the trench and run it through the tee and up to the box.

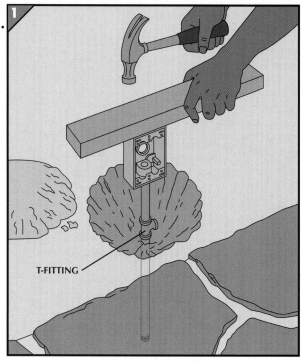

T-FITTING

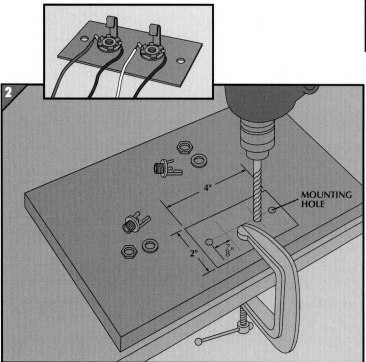

4"

2"

$\frac{7}{8}$"

MOUNTING HOLE

## 2. Making an adapter plate.
To support speaker jacks inside the box, adapt a standard blank switch plate.

◆ Trim the plate to 2 by 4 inches with tin snips.

◆ Mark a line between the mounting holes and an intersecting line $\frac{7}{8}$ inch from each hole.

◆ Clamp the plate to a scrap board on a work surface and drill a $\frac{3}{8}$-inch hole at each intersecting line *(left)*.

◆ Mount speaker jacks in the drilled holes.

◆ Solder a 6-inch length of white wire to the spring-contact terminal of the upper jack, a red wire to the spring-contact terminal of the lower jack, and a black wire to the remaining terminal on each jack *(inset)*.

## 3. Mounting the adapter plate.
◆ With wire caps, connect the wires from the speaker jacks to the matching wires of the three-conductor cable in the electrical box.

◆ Drill new mounting holes in a standard outdoor-receptacle cover and its gasket, using the adapter plate as a template for the drill bit.

◆ Screw the three pieces to the box with 1-inch machine screws.

◆ Inside the house, connect the three-conductor cable to the amplifier *(page 95)*.

◆ Outdoors, plug the left speaker into the upper jack and the right speaker into the lower jack.

◆ Backfill the trench with dirt.

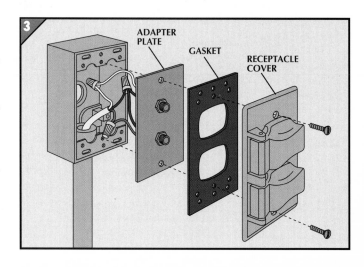

ADAPTER PLATE

GASKET

RECEPTACLE COVER

# Wiring for a Multitude of Speakers

**D**riving two main speakers and three or more pairs of remote speakers from one amplifier requires a distribution system. The setup shown here employs electronic devices called audio transformers and line transformers between the amp and the speakers.

**Sizing Components:** The wattage of the transformers and speakers must match that of the amp. A 100-watt amp, for example, would require audio and line transformers with a rating of 70-volts/100-watts, and speakers whose total wattage does not exceed 100.

**Wiring Line Transformers:** A line transformer has two sets of terminals: The primary, or input, terminals receive the signal from the amp; and the secondary, or output, terminals send it on to the speakers. A 100-watt model has primary terminals for 0.63, 1.25, 2.5, 5, and 10 watts; and secondary terminals rated 4, 8, and in some models, 16 ohms. The terminals you use depend on the ohms and minimum-wattage ratings of the speakers, usually indicated on the back of the speakers or in the owner's manual. For example, 8-ohm speakers requiring a minimum of 5 watts would connect to the line transformer's 5-watt primary and 8-ohm secondary terminals. If the wattage requirement falls between two terminal ratings, use the terminal with the lower rating. Make sure the total wattage of the primary terminals you intend to use does not exceed the amp's maximum output rating.

 **TOOLS**

Soldering iron
Long-nose pliers
Screwdriver
Electric drill
Multipurpose tool

 **MATERIALS**

Stereo speakers
70-volt line and audio transformers
Three-conductor cable

Volume controls
Solder
Sheet-metal screws (No. 8)
Grommets ($\frac{7}{16}$")
Wire caps
Electronics utility box

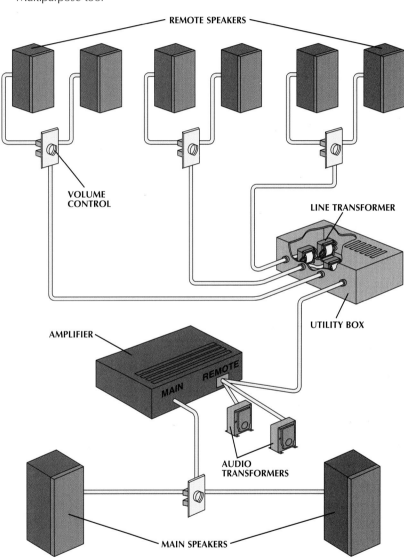

## Anatomy of a distribution system.

In this multiple-speaker system, a pair of audio transformers is wired to the remote-speaker terminals on the back of the amp. The audio transformers convert the amp's output into a form that can be used by the line transformers—also connected to amp's remote-speaker terminals. The line transformers—arranged together inside an electronics utility box—convert and distribute the signal to the speakers. Individual controls regulate the volume of the remote and the main speakers.

# INSTALLING THE TRANSFORMERS

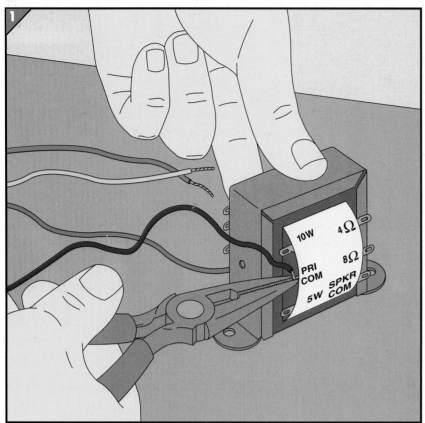

## 1. Wiring the transformers.

◆ Tin the end of a 12-inch-long black wire *(page 92, Step 2)*, loop the lead through the transformer terminal marked PRI COM or C with a pair of long-nose pliers *(left)*, then solder it to the terminal.

◆ Solder a red wire of the same length to the primary terminal marked for the minimum wattage required by each speaker.

◆ Solder a yellow wire 6 inches long to the secondary terminal marked SPEAKER COMMON or SPKR COM, and a 6-inch blue lead to the secondary terminal matching the speaker's ohm rating (usually 8 ohms, or 8 Ω).

◆ Wire the other transformers in the same manner.

◆ Label each transformer with its speaker location and channel—either right or left.

◆ Wind the wires into spirals so they won't become tangled when you secure the transformers to the utility box in Step 2.

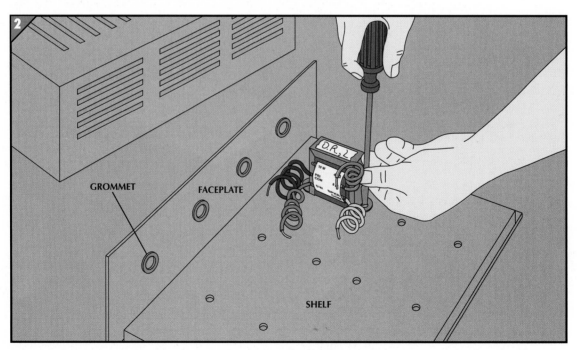

## 2. Adapting a utility box.

◆ If the box does not have predrilled holes for transformers, position the devices on the shelf, arranging each pair in a row. Mark the screw holes, and drill a $\frac{3}{32}$-inch hole at each mark.

◆ For the cables from the audio transformers and speakers, drill a row of evenly spaced $\frac{7}{16}$-inch holes across the middle of the faceplate, offsetting them from the holes in the shelf.

◆ Fit each of the holes in the faceplate with $\frac{7}{16}$-inch grommets.

◆ Fasten each transformer to the shelf with No. 8 sheet-metal screws *(above)*.

## 3. Connecting the amplifier leads.

◆ Run a No. 18 or 16 three-conductor, long enough to reach the amplifier, into a grommeted hole at one end of the utility box.

◆ With wire caps, join the red wires of all the left-channel transformers to the white wire, the red wires of all the right-channel transformers to the red wire, and all the black transformer leads to the black wire, as shown at right.

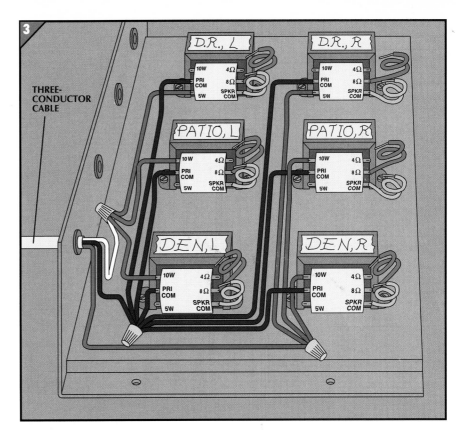

## 4. Completing the wiring.

◆ Run a three-conductor cable from each remote volume control to the utility box and feed the cable through the grommet closest to the appropriate transformer. At each pair of transformers, use wire caps to join the white lead to the blue lead of the left-channel unit, the red lead to the blue lead of the right-channel unit, and the black lead to the yellow leads from both transformers.

◆ At the amplifier, wire a 70-volt audio transformer to each remote-speaker terminal (inset), following the manufacturer's instructions: Here, the green and black wires from each transformer join the positive terminals, and the matching ohms wires—white for 8 ohms— are secured to the negative terminals; the ends of the unused ohms wires are taped. At the same terminals, attach the cable from the utility box as you would a cable from a volume control (page 96).

◆ Connect the wires at the speakers and volume controls (pages 95-96).

# Expanding Your Phone System

Having two telephone lines for one home was once considered a luxury, but with the advent of the home office and its need for separate voice, fax, and modem lines, three and even four lines under one roof has become commonplace.

**Wires and Accessories:** The cable that connects service to jacks is called telephone station wire. Inside its insulation are pairs of colored conductors; each pair serves one phone number. Older systems generally employ quad wire, which has two pairs of straight, or untwisted, conductors. Quad wire is adequate for voice transmission, but a newer product containing twisted conductors comes in several bandwidths and provides more reliable service for fax machines and modems.

**Adding a Second Line:** In most houses, jacks installed by the phone company are wired to serve two phone lines, and sometimes all that is needed to activate the second line at the existing jacks is to order the service from your provider. If you want such a jack to provide only one of the two lines, the procedure is

simple: Open the jack and detach the pair of wires linking the cover plate to the base that correspond to the line you wish to disconnect. Wrap the loose wires with electrical tape and replace the cover.

**Bringing in Multiple Lines:** If you need more than one extra phone number, it is probably best to install new wiring and jacks, especially if the new lines will serve modems or fax machines. Running new wires for a telephone system is no more difficult than extending low-voltage circuits *(pages 84-87)*. How you design the layout is a matter of personal preference, but a home-run wiring scheme *(below)* provides the most versatility.

When you order multiple lines, the phone company usually has a technician run cable for the new phone numbers from the telephone pole to the house and install a box called a network interface *(opposite, top)*. To access these lines, you will need to attach wires to the network interface and route them into the house to a connecting block and jacks *(opposite, bottom)*.

**TOOLS**

Screwdriver
Punch-down tool

**MATERIALS**

Electrical tape
Four-pair twisted
   telephone wire
Telephone wire for
   outdoor use
Connecting block
Modular telephone
   jacks

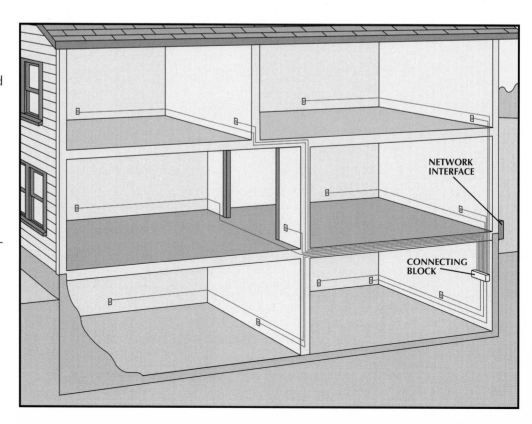

**A versatile layout.**
Up until about 1980, all the jacks in a house were linked in one continuous circuit, a design called series wiring. But in a home-run wiring scheme *(right)*, wires from the network interface run to a connecting block, and each jack in the house is linked to the block by a separate run of wire. Though more time-consuming to install than a series system, this design provides greater flexibility, since you need only switch the point where a jack is fastened to the connecting block to change the phone number serving the jack.

NETWORK INTERFACE

CONNECTING BLOCK

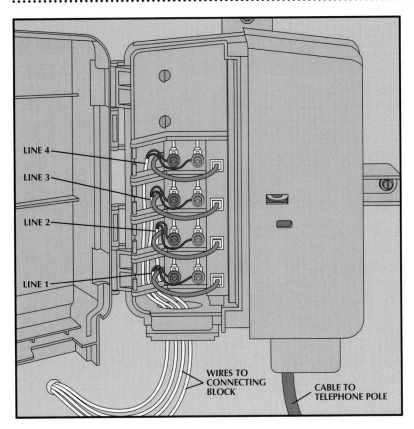

LINE 4
LINE 3
LINE 2
LINE 1

WIRES TO
CONNECTING
BLOCK

CABLE TO
TELEPHONE POLE

## A network interface.

This device is basically a point of connection between the phone company and your house. Designs of network interfaces differ depending on the manufacturer, but inside the box are sets of terminals that correspond to specific phone numbers—the example at left has terminals for four different phone lines. (If more than four lines were needed, a telephone technician would install additional terminals in the remaining space.) A pair of colored conductors of a twisted-wire cable suitable for outdoor use is attached to each set of terminals and, from there, the wire runs into the house to a connecting block and on to the jacks.

## Wiring the connecting block and jacks.

Several models of connecting blocks and jacks are made for home use, but the most versatile type—available at telephone-equipment stores—can provide from one to four lines at every jack. The devices have sets of "ports" instead of the screw terminals found on older equipment, and they are designed to be used in a home-run layout (opposite).

◆ To wire each jack to serve a separate phone number, strip $1\frac{1}{2}$ inches of insulation from the incoming phone lines and untwist the colored conductors.

◆ Place a colored conductor from the first phone line on the appropriate port of the connecting block, as specified by the manufacturer, and press the wire into the port with the punch-down tool, then press the second conductor of the pair into the other port of the set.

◆ Repeat the procedure with the rest of the incoming lines, inserting their conductors into the appropriate ports of each set (right, top). (Sets of ports are shown here separated by blue lines.)

◆ Run a length of four-pair twisted wire with a modular plug at one end from each outlet on the connecting block to each jack and, with the

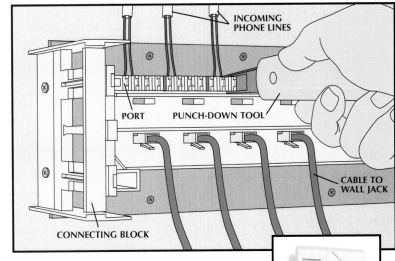

INCOMING
PHONE LINES

PORT    PUNCH-DOWN TOOL

CABLE TO
WALL JACK

CONNECTING BLOCK

punch-down tool, attach all four pairs of conductors to the jacks (photograph).

To provide two phone lines at one jack, attach both lines to the set of ports that serves the jack. To provide all four lines at all the jacks, strip off 10 inches of insulation from the incoming lines and attach all four pairs of colored conductors to the first set of ports; then run the excess length of each conductor in a snake-like fashion through a corresponding port in each of the other five sets.

# Installing a Satellite Dish

**M**odern satellite television systems operate by collecting digital signals broadcast from satellites hovering in orbit above the earth. To view the signals on your TV set, you need to install the components to receive them, and subscribe to one of the commercial providers that send the signals to the satellites. To save money, you can set up these components yourself, but check your local building and electrical codes first, as some areas may prohibit the mounting of exterior satellite dishes.

**Locating the Dish:** The best location for a satellite dish is a house wall, high enough to clear most obstructions—including tree branches and leaves—but as close to the receiver inside the house as possible, so that you need no more than 100 feet of coax cable between the dish and the receiver. Consult the manufacturer's guide to determine the ideal location for your model, but in general, leave room for adjusting the dish, and choose a site free of obstructions between the dish and the southern sky—the location of all satellites serving TVs in the Northern Hemisphere. Once the dish is properly aligned with the appropriate satellite, you will not need to move it again.

Mount the dish on a solid surface such as brick, concrete block, or a stud, to prevent winds from moving it and affecting the signal. If possible, avoid a wall with aluminum or vinyl siding. Make sure you will be able to reach the dish to brush off snow and remove leaves and other debris.

 **CAUTION** *Do not mount a satellite dish near power lines— and avoid touching any while installing the dish assembly.*

 **TOOLS**

Stud finder
Electric drill
Carpenter's level

Socket wrench
Hammer
Screwdriver

 **MATERIALS**

Satellite dish and installation kit
Sealing compound

 **SAFETY TIPS**

*Wear goggles when driving nails or operating an electric drill.*

## Anatomy of a digital broadcast system.

A typical system consists of a dish-shaped antenna that collects the TV signal and directs it to a feedhorn, which channels the signal through coax cable to a receiver inside the house. The dish assembly is attached to the house wall by a mounting bracket. A mast rises from the bracket and joins a support-arm assembly, to which the dish and feedhorn are attached. At the base of the wall is fastened a grounding block that links two sections of TV coax cable to the house's ground through a separate wire. From the grounding block, one cable runs up the wall and through a hole in the mast to the support arm, where it is connected to the feedhorn; another length of cable goes from the grounding block to the receiver. The cable and ground wire are held against the house wall with coax-cable clips.

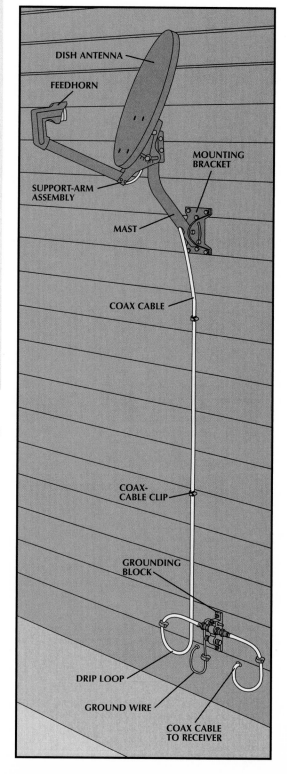

DISH ANTENNA
FEEDHORN
MOUNTING BRACKET
SUPPORT-ARM ASSEMBLY
MAST
COAX CABLE
COAX-CABLE CLIP
GROUNDING BLOCK
DRIP LOOP
GROUND WIRE
COAX CABLE TO RECEIVER

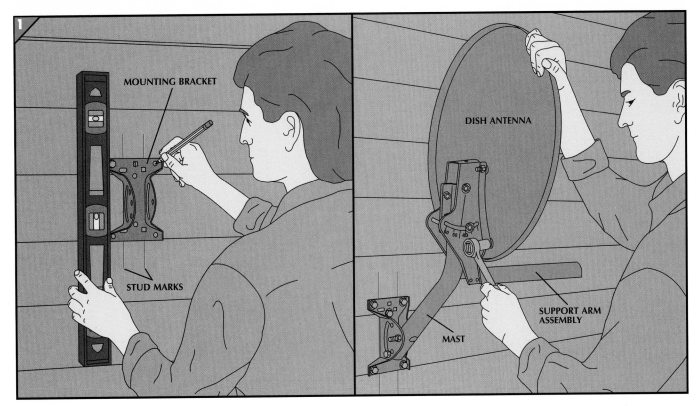

## 1. Putting up the dish.

◆ To install the dish on siding, locate and mark the stud to which the mounting bracket will be attached.

◆ Center the bracket over the stud and mark its upper left hole.

◆ Drill a pilot hole at the mark for the lag screw included in the installation kit, then fasten the plate to the wall through the hole.

◆ Plumb the bracket with a carpenter's level and mark the remaining screw holes on the wall *(above, left)*.

◆ Drill pilot holes at the marks, then attach the bracket to the stud and wall through the remaining holes.

◆ Fasten the support-arm assembly to the mast with the bolt provided, then attach the dish antenna to the support-arm assembly with the nuts and bolts in the kit *(above, right)*.

For a masonry wall, attach the mounting bracket with the anchors and machine bolts supplied with the kit.

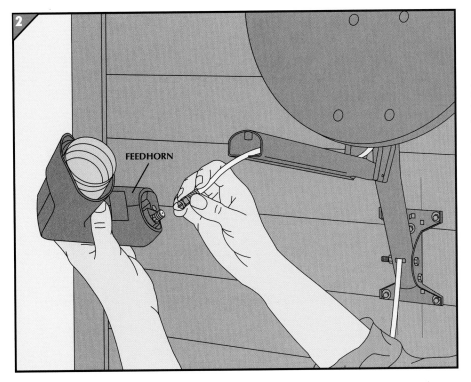

## 2. Hooking up the feedhorn.

◆ Run the TV coax cable provided in the kit up through the hole in the mast and through the support arm.

◆ Screw the cable to the feedhorn *(left)*, then fasten the feedhorn to the support arm with the screw included.

## 3. Aiming the dish.

◆ Using the compass provided by the dish manufacturer, point the dish due south *(right)*.

◆ Inside the house, hook up the receiver to the television and run the telephone wire included in the kit into a phone jack. Punch your zip code into the remote-control keypad—an elevation reading for your location will appear on the TV screen.

◆ Back outside, loosen the bolt holding the support arm assembly to the mast and following the elevation numbers on the assembly, set it to the proper position.

◆ Retighten the bolt *(inset)*.

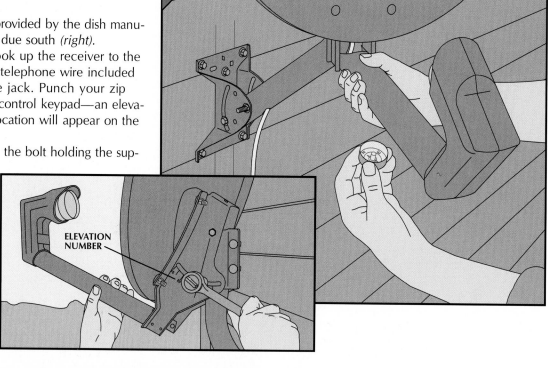

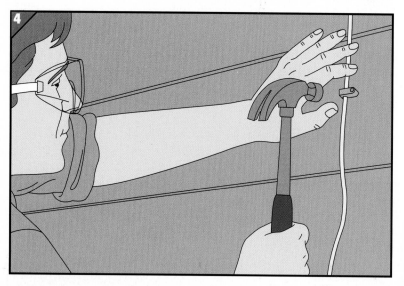

ELEVATION
NUMBER

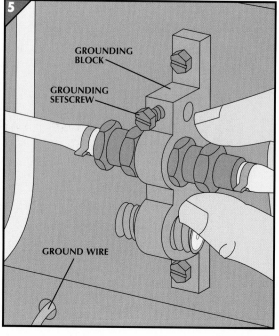

GROUNDING
BLOCK

GROUNDING
SETSCREW

GROUND WIRE

## 4. Running the cable.

At 4-foot intervals along a wood-siding wall, secure the cable with coax-cable clips and the supplied nails *(left)*; for a masonry wall, fasten the clips with the supplied anchors and screws.

## 5. Grounding the cable.

◆ Screw the grounding block to a wall stud or fasten it with masonry anchors near the point where you will bring the cable indoors. Drill a $\frac{1}{4}$-inch hole through the wall near the grounding block and feed the ground wire through the hole.

◆ Beside the grounding block, form a drip loop with the coax cable from the feedhorn to prevent moisture from running into the block. Attach the cable to one of the top terminals on the grounding block. If the cable is too long, cut it to length and attach an F-connector to the end *(page 89)*.

◆ Form another drip loop with a second length of coax cable and connect it to the free top terminal *(right)*.

◆ Run the grounding wire to the house's grounding system *(pages 57-59)* and attach the other end to the grounding block by threading it through the hole and tightening the grounding setscrew.

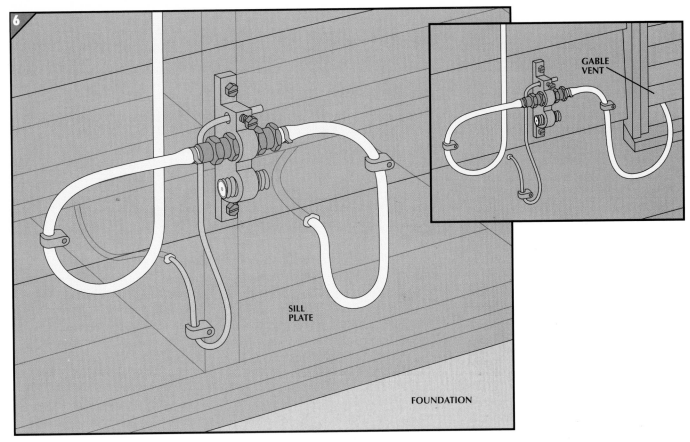

**GABLE VENT**

**SILL PLATE**

**FOUNDATION**

## 6. Bringing the cable indoors.

◆ Route the coax cable from the grounding block through a $\frac{1}{2}$-inch hole drilled through the siding 4 or 5 inches above the sill plate on the foundation wall *(above)* or through a hole in a window frame. If you are bringing the cable into an attic, you can route it through the bottom louver of a gable vent *(inset)*.

◆ Run the cable to the receiver at the television set, keeping the wiring at least 2 inches away from any current-carrying lines.
◆ Connect the receiver to the TV following the manufacturer's instructions.
◆ Outside, fill any holes you drilled with sealing compound, available at electrical-supply stores.

### TRICKS OF THE TRADE

### Fine-Tuning the Dish

Once a dish is set to its prescribed position, you should receive a clear picture on the TV set. During bad weather, however, the picture quality may deteriorate. To adjust the dish to find the strongest signal—a good idea immediately following installation and every six months thereafter—you can purchase a special fine-tuner. To hook up the tuner, disconnect the coax cable from the feedhorn and attach it to the terminal at the top of the tuner, then disconnect the cable attached to the grounding block and hook it up to the terminal at the bottom. Turn the tuner on and move the dish back and forth a little at a time until the tuner indicates optimal signal strength. Reconnect the cables to the feedhorn and grounding block.

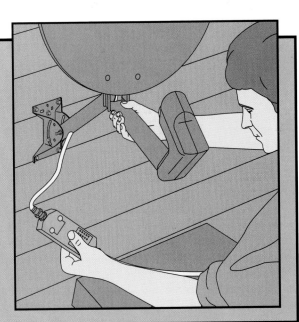

# Mounting a Rooftop TV Antenna

Always popular in rural areas, TV antennas are also practical for city dwellers with satellite dishes who want to pick up the local channels that are unavailable with a dish. You can install a new antenna yourself, or simply improve an existing setup by replacing twin-lead wires with coax cable or grounding the system.

**Choosing the Right Kind:** Antennas come in a variety of shapes and sizes *(below)*. Some pick up a single channel; others pick up VHF (channels 2 to 13), UHF (channels 14 to 83), or FM radio channels; and still others receive VHF, UHF, and FM. Whatever its design, an antenna is sized according to its distance from the transmitting stations in the area. It is sold with either mileage-range figures or such ratings as local, suburban, fringe, and far fringe; and its cost increases with its distance rating. Before buying an antenna, con-

sult your dealer on any unusual features of your site: A location in a valley or behind a large building may call for a larger antenna or a higher mast. The size of the antenna may also depend on whether you plan to install a distribution system *(pages 115-116)* to feed several receivers.

**Preparatory Work:** Assemble as much of the unit as possible on the ground before you get up on the roof. Make sure the mounting location is in good repair; if you plan to fasten to a chimney, first make sure it is structurally sound, and repoint any deteriorating mortar joints.

 *Position ladders as far as possible from electrical service wires and be sure that neither the antenna elements nor the mast touch wires as you carry the assembly up to the roof.*

 **TOOLS**

Wrench
Tin snips

Carpenter's level
Plumb bob
Electric drill
Coax-cable crimper

 **MATERIALS**

Antenna and
   mounting kit
Matching
   transformer
Weatherproofing
   compound

F-connectors
Electrical tape
Coax cable
   and clips
Grounding block
Ground wire
Sealing
   compound

**SAFETY TIPS**

*Put on goggles when nailing or using a power tool, and wear work gloves when handling antenna elements. For roof work, don rubber-soled shoes and use a ladder supported by roof hooks over the peak.*

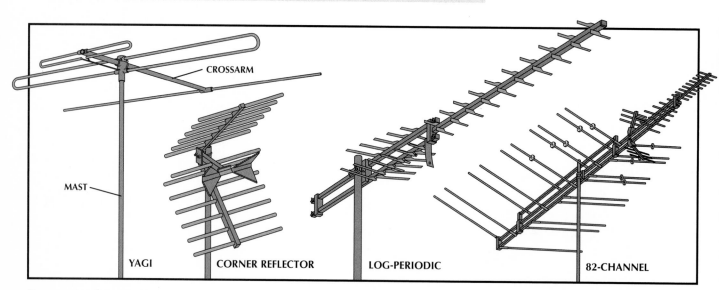

YAGI     CORNER REFLECTOR     LOG-PERIODIC     82-CHANNEL

CROSSARM

MAST

## An array of antennas.

All of the antennas shown above are made of weather-resistant aluminum and have receiving elements arranged on a central crossarm, or boom. The shape and arrangement of the elements indicate the antenna's function. The Yagi antenna uses two looped elements and a straight reflector element to pick up

VHF and the FM radio band. In the corner reflector, a wedge-shaped array of reflectors replaces the straight Yagi reflector and an element in the shape of a bow tie replaces the Yagi loops to form a compact UHF-only antenna. A more sophisticated UHF design called a log-periodic uses a series of successively larger elements that act as reflectors for

each other to strengthen the signal. The large VHF-FM-UHF model called an 82-channel antenna combines a log-periodic UHF section, a corner reflector, and a log-periodic VHF and FM radio section. The plastic disks on the VHF elements are electronic dividers that enable each element to receive the wavelengths of several different channels.

# BRACES FOR THE MAST

### A chimney mount.

◆ Working on the ground, assemble two mounting-strap assemblies. Push the eyebolt at the end of each mounting strap through the hole at the middle of a bracket and secure the bolt with a few turns of the nut *(right, top)*.

◆ Secure a loose eyebolt to the flange at one end of each bracket and a U-bolt to the other end, ensuring that all the nuts are on the same side of the bracket.

◆ On the roof, loop one of the straps around the chimney a foot or so above the roof. Slip a retaining clip over the end of the strap, thread the strap through the second eyebolt, pulling it tight to cinch the bracket to a corner of the chimney *(right, bottom)*.

◆ Feed the end of the strap through the retaining clip, then fold the strap back over the clip toward the bracket and hammer the ends of the clip down over the strap to hold it securely.

◆ Cut off the excess strapping with tin snips, then tighten the nuts on the eyebolts.

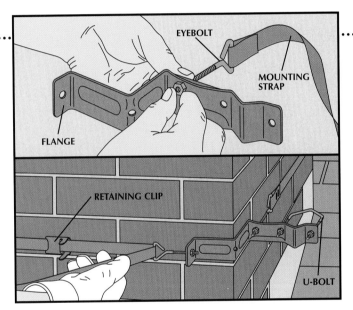

◆ Install the second mounting strap assembly in the same way farther up the chimney—at least one third of the mast length above the first one.

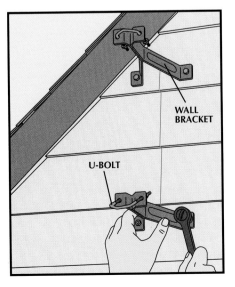

### A wall mount.

◆ Working on the ground, install U-bolts loosely in a pair of wall brackets. For a wall under a wide roof projection, you may need adjustable brackets that can secure a mast up to 18 inches away from the wall.

◆ With a carpenter's level as a guide, draw a plumb line at least one third of the mast length on the wall at the point you have chosen for the antenna.

◆ Center the brackets over the plumb line, one at each end, and mark the holes.

◆ At each mark, drill a pilot hole for the lag screws provided in the antenna-mounting kit.

◆ In line with each pair of holes, secure a 2-by-4 brace inside the attic as for a wall-mounted service entrance *(page 76, Step 4)*.

◆ Fasten the brackets to the braces through the siding and sheathing *(left)*.

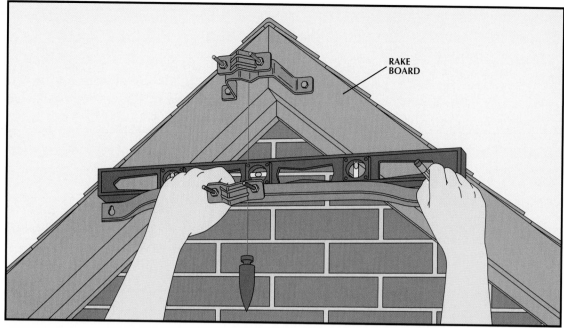

RAKE BOARD

**A gable mount.**

◆ Center and level the upper bracket on the rake boards immediately below the ridge. Mark and drill holes for the lag screws provided with the mounting kit, then fasten the bracket.

◆ Hang a plumb bob from the center of the bracket

and, at a point at least one third of the mast length below the first bracket, align the lower bracket, guided by the plumb line and a level, and mark the holes *(above)*.

◆ Drill pilot holes for the lag shields and screws supplied and fasten the lower bracket in place.

# ASSEMBLING THE ANTENNA

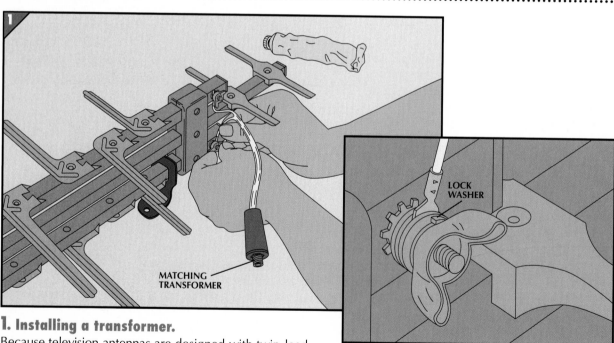

LOCK WASHER

MATCHING TRANSFORMER

**1. Installing a transformer.**

Because television antennas are designed with twin-lead terminals, you will probably have to connect a weatherproof matching transformer to the end of the coax cable to attach the cable to the antenna's twin-lead terminals; some antennas have this transformer already attached.

◆ Working on the ground, loosen the wing nuts of the two connection terminals on the crossarm of the antenna, and

slip the spade connectors of the transformer between the large terminal washers *(inset)*.

◆ Tighten the wing nuts onto the small lock washers *(above)*, and coat each terminal with a weatherproofing compound such as clear silicone sealant or petroleum jelly.

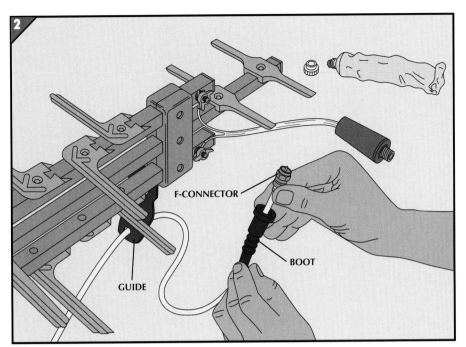

## 2. Connecting the down-lead.

◆ Thread the end of the down-lead cable through any guides on the crossarm and slide the rubber boot supplied with the matching transformer over the end of the coax cable.

◆ Attach an F-connector to the end of the coax cable *(page 89)*.

◆ Force weatherproofing compound into the boot, then screw the connector tightly to the threaded fitting on the transformer and slide the boot over the connector.

F-CONNECTOR

BOOT

GUIDE

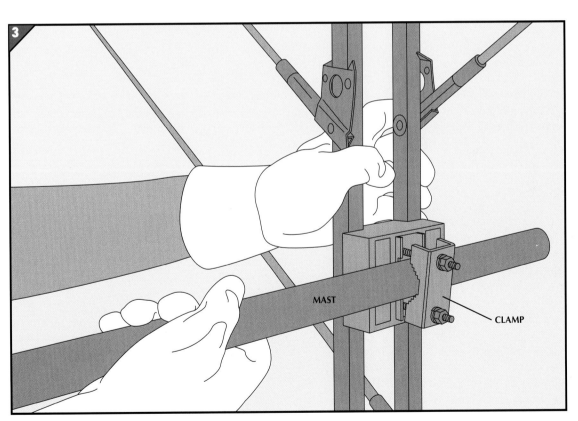

MAST

CLAMP

## 3. Attaching the antenna to the mast.

◆ Unfold the antenna elements until they lock into their fully open position.

◆ Loosen the antenna clamp and slide the mast between its jaws until the top of the mast protrudes a few inches above the antenna *(above)*.

◆ Secure the cable to the top part of the mast with electrical tape, stopping at the part of the mast that will be clamped *(page 114, Step 1)*.

◆ If you are installing a rotator *(pages 117-121)*, fasten it to the mast now.

# COMPLETING THE JOB

## 1. Mounting the antenna.

◆ Slide the end of the mast through the loose clamp assemblies of the antenna mounts *(near right)*.

◆ Tighten the nuts on the U-bolts until the clamps hold the mast firmly in place without crushing it *(far right)*.

◆ Fasten the cable to the lower part of the mast with electrical tape.

◆ Run the cable along the roof and down the house wall, stopping near the point at which it will enter the house—through the siding 4 to 5 inches above the foundation, through the louvers of a gable vent, or through a hole in a window frame. Fasten the cable to the wall with coax-cable clips *(page 108, Step 4)*.

◆ Screw a coax grounding block to the wall near the cable's entry point *(page 108, Step 5)*.

◆ Leaving enough cable to create a drip loop at the grounding block, cut it and attach an F-connector to the end *(page 89)*.

◆ Fasten the cable to a terminal in the grounding block and ground it. If you have installed a rotator, protect the leads with a device called an antenna discharger *(page 120, Step 6)*, available at electrical-supply stores.

## 2. Bringing the cable indoors.

◆ Attach coax cable to the grounding-block terminal opposite the down-lead cable from the antenna, form a drip loop, and run it indoors *(page 108, Step 5)*.

◆ Fill any holes in the siding with sealing compound.

◆ Indoors, run the wire to the television or splitter location *(pages 85-87)*, keeping the cable at least 2 inches from current-carrying lines.

◆ Screw the coax cable into the input coax terminal on the back of the television or VCR. If your set lacks this terminal, screw the UHF and VHF leads of a matching transformer with separate UHF and VHF outputs to the corresponding terminals on the back of the television *(right)*. Attach the coax cable from the grounding block to the coax terminal on the transformer, then mount the transformer on the back panel of the television with the adhesive supplied by the manufacturer.

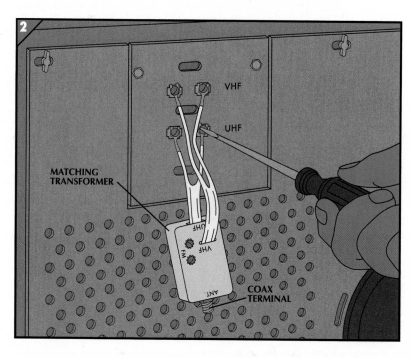

For a home with multiple televisions, an antenna distribution system multiplies the value of an outside antenna, and is far easier to install than the antenna that feeds it. From a single antenna and coax down-lead, the distribution setup can send signals to several TV sets, VCRs, or stereos, or to several outlets for a portable television.

If your house is served by a community antenna and a cable, check with the cable company before you put in a system; for a nominal charge, some companies will install one for you—even to the point of snaking wires inside the walls. Otherwise, install your own system, fitted to your special needs.

**Splitting the Signal:** The simplest arrangement consists of a two- or four-way signal splitter, usually located in the basement or attic, feeding the signal from a large antenna to two to four sets *(below)*. The leads that carry the signal can be brought through floors, or fished through the walls to permanent wall outlets *(page 116)*. At each outlet, a distribution lead from the signal splitter goes to a coax connector on the back of a wall plate; a short coax lead carries the signal to the set from a connector on the front of the plate.

**Boosting the Signal:** A four-way splitter feeds four sets, but in a location more than 15 miles from a transmitter, a single antenna may not be able to supply four TV receivers. (Even two sets may be too many in fringe areas.) The solution is an amplifier that boosts the strength of the signal *(page 116)*; these devices are available for VHF, UHF, or 82-channel amplification and can create a signal strong enough to feed as many as 16 outlets. The model you choose may have a built-in signal splitter or may come with a single output terminal that must be hooked to a separate splitter.

Unfortunately, an amplifier can create new problems: With its signal boosted, a strong local TV or FM station may overpower weaker stations. Here, the solution consists of traps *(page 116)*. These devices reduce the strength of troublesome signals; some models can also eliminate outside interference such as CB- or ham-radio transmissions.

**TOOLS**

Screwdriver
Coax-cable crimper
Keyhole saw
Electric drill
Fish tape

**MATERIALS**

Signal splitter
Coax cable and
   connectors
Matching
   transformer
DC blocking
   terminator
Coax wall outlets
Signal amplifier
FM or VHF trap

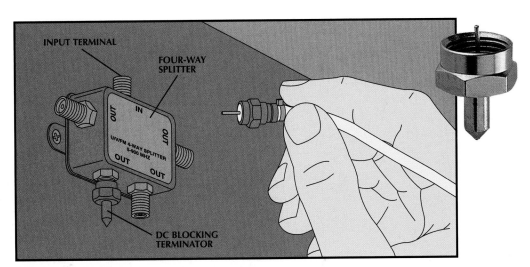

### Installing a signal splitter.

◆ In an inconspicuous location such as a basement, attic, or closet, screw a two- or four-way splitter to a joist or other structural member and attach the antenna down-lead to the input terminal *(above)*.

◆ Run coax leads from the output terminals to the coax input terminal on each TV or to a wall outlet *(page 116)*. For older TV sets without coax inputs, attach each lead to a matching transformer connected to the set's UHF and VHF terminals *(opposite, Step 2)*.

◆ Cap each unused output terminal with a DC blocking terminator *(photograph)*, available in antenna or electronics stores.

## Mounting a coax wall outlet.

◆ Choose a location for a wall outlet and cut a hole $1\frac{3}{4}$ inches wide and 4 inches high in the wall with a keyhole saw.

◆ Fish the coax cable from the splitter through the hole.

◆ Screw the front and back straps of the outlet brackets loosely together, slip the back straps behind the wall with their central mounting holes $3\frac{3}{4}$ inches apart, and tighten the screws to clamp the brackets in place *(right)*. If you plan to add an antenna rotator *(pages 117-121)*, use wall plates fitted with receptacles for the rotator cable *(page 120, Step 7)*.

◆ Attach the cable to the connector on the back of the wall plate and screw the plate to the brackets.

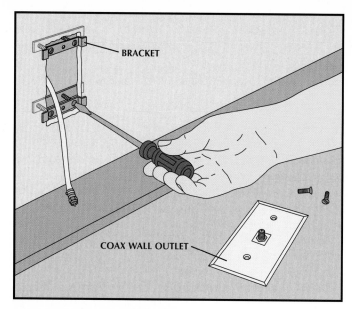

BRACKET

COAX WALL OUTLET

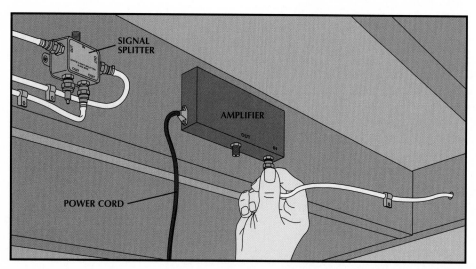

SIGNAL SPLITTER

AMPLIFIER

OUT

IN

POWER CORD

## Adding an amplifier.

◆ Mount a signal amplifier near the splitter at a point where its power cord can be plugged in or wired into the 120-volt house current.

◆ Attach the antenna down-lead to the input terminal of the amplifier *(left)*, and run coax cable from the amplifier output to the input terminal of a signal splitter or to the coax input or matching transformer on a TV set.

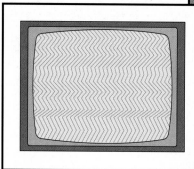

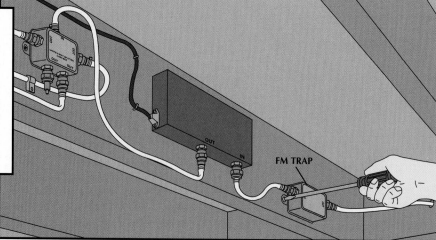

FM TRAP

## Correcting overloads.

To eliminate interference from a strong FM signal—often indicated by a herringbone pattern on the TV screen *(inset)* or a completely scrambled picture—wire an FM trap between the antenna down-lead and the amplifier input, then mount the trap *(above)*. You can still run the antenna signal to an FM radio by installing a TV/FM band separator between the antenna and the trap, and by running a cable from the separator to the FM set.

To get rid of overload from a local TV station, indicated by a negative image or by a series of vertical black bars that drift across the screen, wire a single-channel VHF trap for the offending channel into the down-lead as you would an FM trap.

# A Rotator to Aim an Antenna

**M**ost television antennas work best when they face a transmitter squarely—that is, when the front of the boom (normally, the end that supports the short elements) points toward the television station. Receptivity falls off and colors wash out if the antenna points away from the signal source—a swing of 30 degrees will spoil any picture; a smaller swing will ruin reception if you use a complex antenna or tune your TV to a high-number channel.

**Aiming an Antenna:** With a rotator, you can turn the boom of the antenna in the right direction, and scan the horizon for incoming signals. In locations between cities, the antenna can swing to capture signals from transmitters that lie in opposite directions. In fringe areas it can find stations up to 100 miles away with an accuracy of 5 degrees or less—a degree of precision that can make the difference between a clear picture and a snowy one. When a TV picture is spoiled by ghosting (a double image created by a combination of direct signals and signals that are reflected off nearby hillsides or large buildings),

the rotator can turn the antenna away from the ghost or, sometimes, deliberately choose it. And if you tune in to UHF channels between 14 and 68, a rotator is even more valuable, for UHF transmitters are likely to be widely scattered.

**A Remote-Control Rotor:** A typical unit consists of two parts: a control box, placed near the set; and a rotor, mounted on the antenna mast in a weatherproof housing. The control activates a transformer that converts the 120-volt current from a wall plug into a 24-volt current. From the control box, a lightweight cable carries the low-voltage current to the motor through circuits that turn the transformer off after the antenna has turned to a new position. For added protection, a grounded lightning arrester, called a discharger, is installed on the rotator cable *(page 120, Step 6)*. If your antenna has a flat, twin-lead connection, switch to a coax lead-in cable *(page 113, Step 2)* when you install a rotator; the cable will complement the rotator in improving reception.

 **TOOLS**

Screwdriver
Multipurpose tool
Hacksaw
Wrench

 **MATERIALS**

Rotator kit
Electrical tape

 **SAFETY TIPS**

*Goggles protect your eyes when you are cutting through metal.*

---

## OPERATING AN ANTENNA ROTATOR

With the rotator at rest, the control-knob indicator dot of this typical control box lines up with the point on the compass rim that matches the direction of the antenna. When you turn the knob to another compass point, the rotor will turn the antenna. The indicator dot will move as well, following the direction of antenna rotation. When the antenna reaches the new orientation, the antenna and indicator will automatically stop, and the control unit will switch off. In the rotator shown here, a control-box motor synchronized to the rotor turns the indicator. Because continuous rotation would twist the antenna lead until it snapped, the rotor and control knob reach a stop point after a maximum of one full revolution in either direction. In the synchronous-motor system shown here, the antenna is installed facing north at its stop point *(inset)*; if this direction lies between much-used channels, you can reinstall the antenna *(pages 110-114)* so it faces south at the stop point and relabel the compass points on the control panel to match the directions of the antenna.

CONTROL KNOB

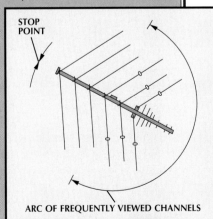

STOP POINT

ARC OF FREQUENTLY VIEWED CHANNELS

# INSTALLING THE ROTATOR

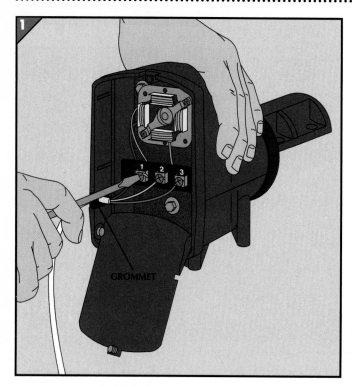

## 1. Connecting the rotor wires.

◆ Unscrew and open the door on the bottom of the rotor.
◆ Strip about $1\frac{1}{2}$ inches of the outer insulation *(page 19)* from the rotator-control cable supplied in the kit. Separate the leads and strip about $\frac{1}{2}$ inch of insulation from each one.
◆ Remove the grommet from the wire slot, insert the cable through the hole in the grommet, and press it back in place.
◆ Connect the wires to the terminals *(left)*. The rotator shown here contains three wires; other models may have four. Note the terminal number to which each wire is connected; you will need to match the cable wires and their terminal numbers on the control box *(page 121, Step 8)*.
◆ Screw the rotor door back into place.

## 2. Mounting the mast to the rotor.

◆ Disconnect the coax down-lead from the antenna, then detach the antenna and mast and bring them down from the roof.
◆ With a hacksaw, cut through the mast by the distance below the antenna specified by the rotator manufacturer.
◆ Attach the mast to the mast-support section of the rotor with the mounting brackets supplied, so the cut end extends slightly beyond the bottom bracket *(right)*.

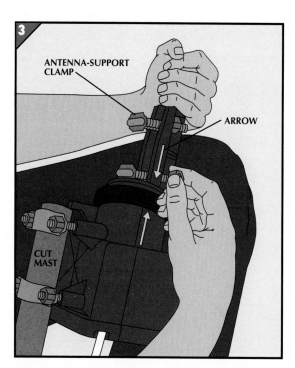

## 3. Preparing the rotor for the antenna.

◆ Check that the arrows on the mast- and antenna-support sections of the rotor are aligned; if they are not, connect the cable to the control box *(page 121, Step 8)* and rotate the antenna-support section from the box until the arrows line up.
◆ Install the antenna-support clamps on the rotor *(left)*, leaving them loose enough to set the antenna in position in the rotor.
◆ Remount the mast and rotor assembly on the roof *(page 114, Step 1)*.

## 4. Orienting the antenna.

◆ Slide the antenna through the clamps on the rotor so the bottom sits flush on the housing.

◆ Rotate the mast until the front of the antenna points north or south, as directed in the instruction sheet supplied by the manufacturer or according to the locations of nearby TV transmitters *(page 117, box)*.

◆ Tighten the nuts on the clamps enough to keep the antenna from slipping *(left)*.

## 5. Leading the wires down.

◆ Reconnect the coax down-lead to the antenna and tape it to the mast with electrical tape, leaving enough slack above the tape to allow the antenna to turn 360 degrees without binding *(right)*.

◆ Tape the rotator control cable to the mast every 3 to 4 feet.

DOWN-LEAD

ROTATOR-CONTROL CABLE

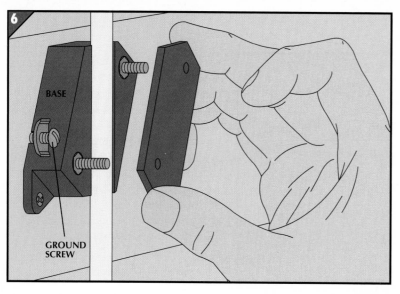

BASE

GROUND
SCREW

## 6. Installing a discharger.

To provide additional protection in the event the rotor is struck by lightning, you can ground the device.

◆ Remove the cover of a rotator static-and-lightning discharger and fasten the base to the roof or wall of the house near the entry point of the rotator cable.

◆ Run the cable through the discharger's central channel, then replace the cover *(left)*.

◆ Run a ground wire from the discharger's ground screw to the house ground *(pages 57-59)*.

◆ Run the rotator cable into the house through the antenna down-lead opening.

## 7. Connections to wall plates.

For a control box that you do not expect to move, wire the rotator cable directly to the box *(opposite, Step 8)*.

◆ If you have several outlets for antenna connections *(page 116)*, replace them with wall plates fitted with receptacles for the rotator cable.

◆ Run the rotator cable from plate to plate, making connections at screw terminals *(right, top)* or soldering lugs.

◆ Wire a plug for inserting into the wall plates by tracing the terminal-number sequence of the cable through to the holes in the face of the receptacle and, in a matching pattern, connect a cable—long enough to run from the outlet to the control box—to the prongs in the plug base. Slip the cover on the base *(right, bottom)*.

◆ Connect the wires at the other end of the plug cable to the control box *(opposite, Step 8)*, allowing you to plug the box into any of the outlets. Do not plug in additional control boxes unless the rotator you are installing will accept them and do not turn the control knob while moving the box between outlets.

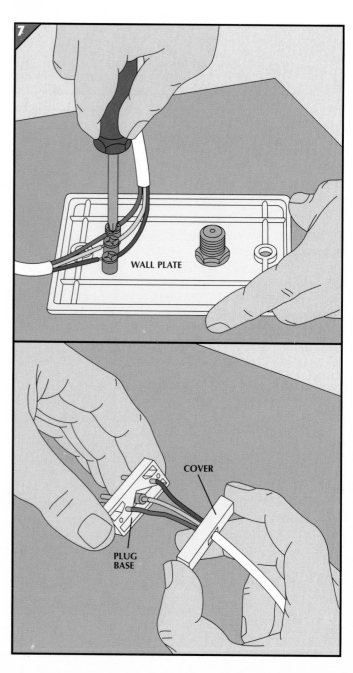

WALL PLATE

COVER

PLUG
BASE

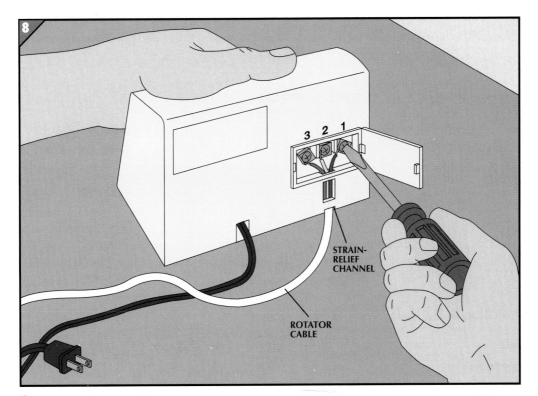

STRAIN-RELIEF CHANNEL

ROTATOR CABLE

### 8. Connections at the control box.
◆ Strip the control-box end of the rotator cable as for the rotor end *(page 118, Step 1)*.
◆ Run the cable through the strain-relief channel on the bottom of the control box and connect it to the terminals, matching the wires to the same terminal numbers as the rotor *(above)*.

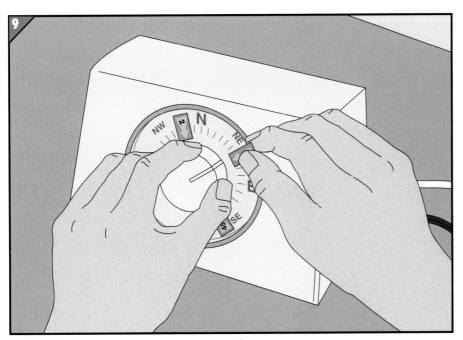

### 9. Marking the channels.
◆ Test the rotator setup by turning the knob on the control unit clockwise as far as it will go. If you set up the antenna to face north, when the antenna has reached the end of its rotation, the indicator dot should be pointing south. Now turn it in the counterclockwise direction; the dot should indicate north. If you obtain different results from either test, refer to the manufacturer's instructions to synchronize the control unit and rotor.
◆ Select a channel on the TV, then rotate the control knob to the position on the dial that provides the best reception. Label this position on the dial with the channel sticker provided with the rotator *(left)*.

# Appendix

**4**

To determine whether a new cable is large enough or a new circuit will overload a service panel, most electricians use a few general rules of thumb. When in doubt, they sometimes put in components that are larger than necessary. You can obtain precise results by referring to the information and charts in this section, based on the rules and formulas in the National Electrical Code.

# Calculating Loads According to the Code

**W**hen checking the effect of an added circuit, you can take advantage of the fact that the electrical loads in your house do not draw power all at once or at full capacity. Some pairs of appliances—air conditioners and heaters, for example—are never used simultaneously. The National Electrical Code defines such loads as "noncoincident" and allows you to include the larger of them in your calculations and to ignore the smaller one.

**Derating Loads:** Some loads, such as electric ranges and the components of a central-heating system, seldom run at full capacity: The circuit breaker and cable that serve these appliances must be large enough to handle the entire load, but the code lets you discount or "derate" part of the loads when you calculate the total capacity required of the service panel.

Since only a fraction of the lights and appliances in your home draw power at any one time, the code specifies 10,000 watts (or 10 kilowatts) as a basic power requirement and lets you discount 60 percent of the remainder of the load when calculating the total requirement. When deciding on what new circuits to install, allow for these requirements for the various types of circuits.

**General Lighting Circuits:** While the code requires three watts of power per square foot of floor space, it does not limit the number of fixtures and receptacles these circuits serve. In practice a 20-ampere circuit should not supply more than 16 outlets or a 15-ampere circuit

more than 12. The lighting circuits can supply stationary appliances—refrigerators, small air conditioners, and the like—but the sum of the appliance ratings must not exceed half the circuit rating, and no single appliance can exceed 80 percent of the circuit rating. (In Canada lighting circuits are limited to 15 amperes and a total of 12 fixtures and receptacles.)

**Small-Appliance Circuits:** The code requires at least two small-appliance circuits, and most homes have more than two; a circuit generally supplies two or three receptacles. These circuits are designed to serve high-wattage kitchen appliances in a dining room, family room, pantry, or kitchen; they cannot be used to serve receptacles in other rooms or lighting fixtures in any room. The restrictions on large appliances described above apply to small-appliance circuits.

**Special-Purpose Circuits:** The code requires only one special-purpose circuit—a 20-ampere, 120-volt laundry circuit for a washing machine—but most homes have several others, for clothes dryers, refrigerators and freezers, ovens, ranges, air conditioners, and other large appliances. Such circuits can be powered by either 120 volts or 240 volts, and can be wired either directly to an appliance or to a receptacle within 6 feet of the appliance. Generally, each circuit supplies only one appliance. The wire sizes for a variety of appliance amperages are given in the chart on page 124.

# A WIRE FOR EVERY CIRCUIT

| Amperage | Copper Wire Size (AWG) |
|----------|------------------------|
| 15 | No. 14 |
| 20 | No. 12 |
| 30 | No. 10 |
| 40 | No. 8 |
| 55 | No. 6 |
| 70 | No. 4 |

**Choosing the right wire.**
The National Electrical Code requires that you match the rating of a circuit to the size of the wire it serves: A wire that is too small for its load can heat dangerously without tripping the breaker.

# THE RIGHT CABLE FOR EVERY SERVICE

| Service-Panel Amperage | Copper Cable | Aluminum Cable |
|------------------------|--------------|----------------|
| 100 | No. 4 | No. 2 |
| 125 | No. 2 | No. 1/0 |
| 150 | No. 1 | No. 2/0 |
| 200 | No. 2/0 | No. 4/0 |

**Sizing service-entrance cable.**
This chart correlates the rated amperage of a service panel with the size of copper or aluminum cable required to serve it. Copper is expensive but easy to bend and connect; aluminum is much cheaper but far less flexible. Copper wiring is preferred, but if you choose aluminum cable, have a specially trained, licensed electrician do the installation.

In Canada, copper is also preferred, and the requirements differ slightly: No. 2 AWG for 100 amps, No. 1 for 125 amps, No. 1/0 for 150 amps and No. 3/0 for 200 amps.

# BRANCH-CIRCUIT AMPERAGES

| Type of Circuit | Amperage |
|-----------------|----------|
| General lighting | 15 or 20 |
| Small appliance | 20 |
| Clothes washer | 20 |
| Nonmotor appliance | Name-plate rating |
| Motor appliance | 125% of name-plate rating |

**The right amperage for each circuit.**
The National Electrical Code sets minimum capacities for certain circuits, depending on their purpose: general lighting, small appliances, or clothes washers. The code does not specify the amperage for circuits serving large appliances—space heaters, electric ranges, and the like—but the capacity of these circuits must be greater than the amperages indicated on the appliance name plates. For motor-driven appliances such as an air conditioner or a stationary power saw, the amperage is calculated by multiplying the name-plate amperage by 125 percent to allow for the current surge when the motor starts. If a motor-driven appliance drawing 3 amps or more is on a circuit with other devices, this adjustment affects only the largest motor; use the name-plate rating of the others.

# CALCULATING THE LOAD ON A SYSTEM

| | Formula | Example | Result |
|---|---|---|---|
| **Heating and air-conditioning load** | 65% of central electric heat | 65% x 14,000 watts | 9,100 watts |
| | 100% of air-conditioning | 100% of 9,700 watts | 9,700 watts |
| **Other loads** | General lighting—3 watts per square foot | 3,000 sq. ft. x 3 watts | 9,000 watts |
| | Small-appliance circuits—1,500 watts each | 3 circuits x 1,500 watts | 4,500 watts |
| | Laundry circuit 1,500 watts or name-plate rating | 1,200-watt washer | 1,500 watts |
| | Clothes dryer—5,000 watts or name-plate rating | 5,500-watt dryer | 5,500 watts |
| | Other major appliances | 1,200-watt dishwasher<br>4,500-watt water heater<br>7,400-watt range<br>9,500-watt oven | 1,200 watts<br>4,500 watts<br>7,400 watts<br>9,500 watts |
| | **Total of other loads** | | 43,100 watts |
| **Derating the total load** | First 10,000 watts of other load at 100% | 100% of 10,000 watts | 10,000 watts |
| | Remainder of other load at 40% | 40% x 33,100 watts | 13,240 watts |
| | Heating or air-conditioning load, whichever is larger | | 9,700 watts |
| | **Total derated load** | | 32,940 watts |
| **Load in amperes (watts/volts)** | | 32,940 watts ÷ 240 volts | 137 amps |

## Calculating the amperage for a house.

This chart is a work sheet for calculating the electrical demands in a typical home. In the top section of the chart, formulas are used to calculate the wattage of each load. In the bottom section, the wattages are derated using more formulas, and the resulting figures are totaled and converted into amperes, indicating the total demand on the system. If your home has a 120/240-volt service of 100 amps or more, use the chart to calculate the necessary service for your system, substituting your own figures in columns three and four.

In the top section of the chart, find 65 percent of the total number of watts of your electric heating unit (in this case, 14,000). For the central air conditioner, use 100 percent of the wattage (here, 9,700 watts). (If you have fewer than four separately controlled space heaters, treat the sum of their wattages in the same way as central heating; if you have four or more, add all of them to the "other loads" category rather than to the heating load.) For the rest of the circuits,

enter their wattages in this manner: Calculate your home's square footage for the general-lighting circuit requirements, counting all living spaces—including attics and basements and excluding crawl spaces, open porches, and garages—and multiply the resulting number by 3. For the laundry circuit, use 1,500 watts or the name-plate rating of the washing machine, whichever is higher. If you have a clothes-dryer circuit, rate it at either 5,000 watts or 125 percent of the name-plate rating. Under "other major appliances" include the wattages of every major appliance you own and of any additional appliances or circuits you plan to install.

To determine the total electrical demand, use the bottom portion of the chart and add together 100 percent of the first 10,000 watts of "other loads," 40 percent of the remainder of "other loads," and 65 percent of the heating load or 100 percent of the air conditioning, whichever is larger. Divide this figure by 240 volts to convert it into amperes. In this example, the total is 137 amps, and a 150-amp service would be sufficient.

# INDEX